To Walk With A Quiet Mind

Hikes in the Woodlands
Parks and Beaches
of the San Francisco Bay Area

D0963437

A Sierra Club Totebook®

To Walk With A Quiet Mind

Hikes in the Woodlands
Parks and Beaches
of the San Francisco
Bay Area

by Nancy Olmsted
with Stephen Whitney

Photographs by John Hamamura

Sierra Club Books • San Francisco • 1975

The Sierra Club, founded in 1892 by John Muir, has devoted itself to the study and protection of the nation's scenic and ecological resources—mountains, wetlands, woodlands, wild shores and rivers. All Club publications are part of the nonprofit effort the Club carries on as a public trust. There are some 50 chapters coast to coast, in Canada, Hawaii, and Alaska. Participation is invited in the Club's program to enjoy and preserve wilderness everywhere. Address: 530 Bush Street, San Francisco, California 94108.

Library of Congress Cataloging in Publication Data

Olmsted, Nancy, 1927-
    To walk with a quiet mind.

    (A Sierra Club Totebook)
    Bibliography: p.
    Includes index.
    1. Golden Gate National Recreation Area, Calif.—
Description and travel—Tours. 2. Hiking—California—Golden Gate National Recreation Area. 3. Trails—Golden Gate National Recreation Area, Calif. I. Title
F868.S156044   917.94'6'045   75-1053
ISBN 0-87156-125-5

Maps by Daniel Gridley
Production by Charlsen + Johansen & Others
Second Printing, 1976.
Printed in the United States of America

Contents

Introduction

THE SAN FRANCISCO BAY AREA remains one of the most beautiful and amenable metropolitan regions in the world because an enormous amount of open space has been preserved in and around its cities. No matter where you live in the area, nature is at your doorstep. Within a half hour of San Francisco, you can picnic at a secluded beach, trod the ancient duff or primeval forests, gambol through high, rolling meadows overlooking the sea, or sit quietly beside a waterfall in a rocky mountain gorge. That such experiences remain possible in an urban area of 3.5 million people is nothing less than incredible.

In the nine Bay Area counties there are some 200,000 acres of public land open to hiking, boating, picnicking, horseback riding, and other activities. It is set aside in numerous city and county parks, more than a dozen regional parks, over two dozen state parks, and three units of the National Park System. Half of this acreage is concentrated in a single area across the Golden Gate just north of San Francisco in Marin County. Here, more than 100,000 acres form a single contiguous unit that includes the Golden Gate National Recreation Area, Muir Woods National Monument, the Point Reyes National Seashore, several state parks, and the watershed lands of the Marin Municipal Utility District. This book is a guide to the major trails that explore these public lands.

This trail guide was written for the hiker in no hurry, the hiker who loves walking as a means of exploration more than as an end in itself. As a result, this book differs from similar guides in two ways: first, it devotes as much space to describing the natural history of the area as it does the

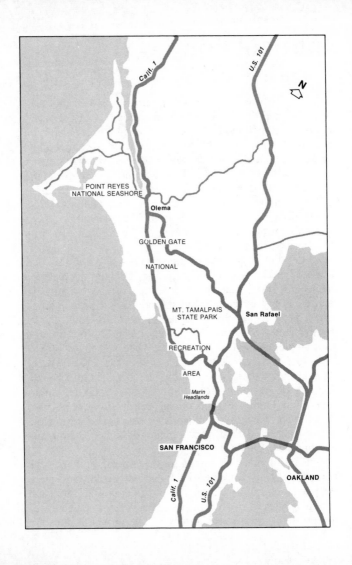

trails themselves; and second, the hikes tend to be either easy or moderate, allowing the average hiker sufficient time to enjoy the natural attractions along the way. The hikes range from short strolls along the seashore to more strenuous loop trips up to nine miles in length. None of them, however, exceed the capability of the average hiker, and many are perfectly suitable for family outings. Each trail description includes some discussion of the more obvious and important natural features to be encountered, and hikers are encouraged to familiarize themselves further with the natural history of the area. A list of field guides to the flora, fauna, and geology of the area is provided in the back of the book.

No attempt was made to include every trail and beach within the area covered by this book. The twenty-seven hikes described here comprise a representative cross-section of those available. They cover virtually all the different types of habitat and terrain to be found within Point Reyes National Seashore and the Golden Gate National Recreation Area—tidepools, sandy beach, sea cliffs and rocky shores, coast grasslands and scrub, oak woodlands, chaparral, coastal evergreen woodlands, bishop pine forest, Douglas fir forest, redwood forest, rocky mountaintops, deep canyons, rolling hillsides, lakes, waterfalls, salt marshes. Because of this diversity of habitat and terrain, the hiker and amateur naturalist will find an equal diversity of flora and fauna. More than 300 species of birds frequent this area during a typical year; mammals include deer, mountain lion, bobcat, badger, raccoon, gray fox, harbor seal, California and Stellar's sea lions, and gray whale; the native flora exceeds 1,000 species and named varieties.

The hikes are grouped into three geographical sections:

the Golden Gate, Mount Tamalpais, and Point Reyes. An introduction to each section describes its geological history, prominent natural features, parks and other public facilities, the best times to visit the area, and the types of trails to be expected. The trail descriptions themselves include specific information about when to go, what to take with you, and how to get to the trailhead. Two generalizations that can be made for almost every trail in this book are: (1) you will usually have to carry your own water, especially during the summer and fall; and (2) you will seldom *need* heavy-soled hiking boots, though they are sometimes preferable to ordinary walking shoes.

The trails included in the Golden Gate section are the closest to San Francisco and will be especially welcome to city residents who have only a morning or afternoon to spare. They include a walk along a secluded San Francisco beach, a trip to Angel Island, and three hikes in the Marin Headlands. All are on lands included within the Golden Gate National Recreation Area.

Mount Tamalpais is situated just a few miles north of the Golden Gate. The hikes in this section explore redwood canyons, grassy knolls overlooking the Pacific, mountain streams and waterfalls, and the top of the peak itself. Most of these trails lie within Muir Woods National Monument, Mount Tamalpais State Park, and Stinson Beach State Park (all of which are independently administered units of the Golden Gate National Recreation Area). Three trails lie within the watershed lands of the Marin Municipal Water District, and one trail explores a privately administered wildlife sanctuary.

All but one of the trails in the Point Reyes section are located on the peninsula itself. Most are within the Point

Reyes National Seashore. These trails explore the wildest country in the Bay Area—virgin forests of Douglas fir, a secluded coastal valley dotted with freshwater lakes, ridgetop meadows, beaches and sand dunes, salt marshes and vast estuaries, deserted grasslands that tumble down from dense forests to the Pacific shore. The Point Reyes Pensinsula, just northwest of Mount Tamalpais, is a one-and-one-half-hour drive from downtown San Francisco.

As you walk the trails in this book, remember that they did not just happen. These lands were set aside because thousands of Bay Area residents cared enough to make sure these areas did not succumb to the bulldozer. The ongoing campaign to preserve the best lands around the bay is a local tradition dating back to the turn of the century. Although conservationists have achieved many of their goals in Marin County, much remains to be done in other parts of the Bay Area. By continuing the great tradition of conservation that has made this the most beautiful metropolitan region in America, it may be possible someday to assure that this beauty will remain forever.

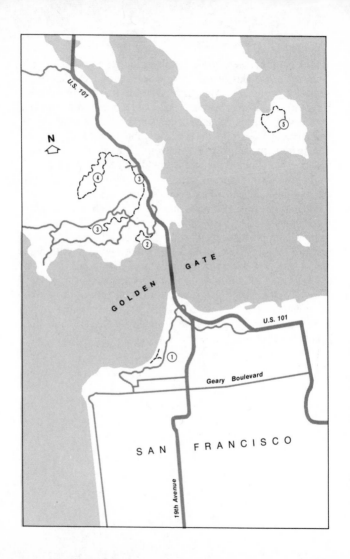

The Golden Gate

THE GOLDEN GATE is one of the most spectacular harbor entrances in the world. Bounded on either side by steep, rocky cliffs, the strait is three miles long and a mile wide. It is like a hallway connecting two large rooms, the Pacific on the west and the 400-square-mile San Francisco Bay on the east. It is one of the only places between the Canadian border and the tip of Baja California—about 2,000 miles—where the ocean has broken the mountain barrier that lines the Pacific Coast. The hills of San Francisco on the south and the steep Marin Headlands on the north are parts of a single mountain block that was first breached by the ancient Sacramento River and later invaded by ocean.

At the close of the Pliocene Epoch—about 2.5 million years ago—the coast of central California was a low, undulating plain. The shore lay far to the west, and the site of the Golden Gate was a vast delta created by the Sacramento River, which drained the country to the east, including the Sierra Nevada. Then, at the beginning of the Pleistocene, the coastal land mass began to break into huge blocks, some of which started to rise. These would become the Coast Range of California and in the Bay Area such familiar landmarks as the Berkeley hills, Tiburon Peninsula, Marin Headlands, and the hills of San Francisco. At this time the bay was still a dry coastal valley, through which the Sacramento River meandered to the sea. But as the ridges began to rise, the river was able to maintain its outlet to the Pacific only by cutting its channel faster than the land could rise to block it. The Golden Gate marks its successful breach of the westernmost ridge. At the close of the last Ice

Age, about 25,000 years ago, the sea level began to rise as meltwater from the world's glaciers returned to its source. The Pacific began to enter the Gate, slowly pushing the Sacramento River eastward and flooding the large valley just beyond the first ridge. This was the beginning of San Francisco Bay; the work was completed 10,000 years ago.

The first European to behold this magnificent harbor may have been Sir Francis Drake, in 1579. But we cannot be sure. His journals have been lost and our only account is somewhat vague on the matter. It is just as likely that Drake missed the narrow entrance to the bay entirely and anchored instead at Drake's Bay a few miles up the coast. It is surely possible that Drake did not discover the Golden Gate, for the Spaniards, who regularly sailed up and down this coast, did not find it for another 200 years. It would seem that so dramatic a breach in the steep cliffs lining most of the coast of northern and central California surely could not escape the attention of these mariners, but it must be remembered that what Drake's chronicler called "stynkinge fogges" often shroud this coast. Even on the clearest days, the Golden Gate is not evident until you are well in toward shore. Today, the surest way to find it is to head for the towers of the Golden Gate Bridge, which mount the narrow strait like the Pillars of Hercules.

If there is one monument that unites the hikes in this section it is the bridge, a structure of such uncommon grace and dignity that it seldom fails to inspire even those who normally scorn the works of man. Old-time Bay Area residents may still feel a rush when they see it from a new angle or in a particularly dramatic light. The bridge is not the focus of the hikes to follow, but its visibility more or less defines the area covered in this section. You can see it from every trail, and each one offers a slightly different perspective on this magnificent monument.

From Baker's Beach and Kirby Cove, which are situated on opposite shores of the Golden Gate, the bridge towers above you to the east. Its 750-foot towers and 6,450-foot span dominate the scene. From the top of the Marin Headlands or the summit of Mount Livermore on Angel Island, you see the bridge in a more vast setting of land and water. But you will be surprised at how little above the tops of the towers you stand. As you traverse Wolfback Ridge on your way down to Rodeo Valley, you can just make out one of the towers poking up behind the distant ridge. While it marks man's intrusion in the otherwise wild landscape, the bridge serves to remind you how fortunate it is that so much open space has been preserved within a fifteen-minute drive of San Francisco.

The Landscape

The chief attraction of these five hikes may be their panoramic views, but when you can shift your attention from the horizon you will discover a landscape of great subtlety. What looks from a distance like a monotonous mantle of grass and low shrubs resolves itself into many complex natural communities, which will reward closer attention. Aside from the predominant grasslands and scrub, you will discover tiny rock gardens of lichen and succulents, moist swales where water seeps down narrow canyons, freshwater marshes lined with sedge and cattails, and streamside willow runs meandering down level valleys. This is a landscape where slight variations in soil, sunlight, steepness of slope, and exposure to the prevailing ocean wind make enormous differences in the type of vegetation you encounter and the particular species of plants that make up each community.

Battered by stiff, salty winds and beleaguered by moist fogs, the ridges that face the Golden Gate and the Pacific are covered largely with hardy grasses and low shrubs. Trees exist only in protected canyons and slopes, primarily on the leeward sides of the coastal ridges, or where they have been planted as buffers against the wind. The pines above Baker's Beach in San Francisco were planted by the army, as were the pines and eucalyptus on Angel Island. Where trees have taken hold in exposed areas, their tops will sweep back toward the east, pruned by the wind to the shape of an airfoil. The wind is strongest through the Golden Gate itself and on the tops of the westernmost ridges. Angel Island is warmer and more protected from the winds because it lies farther away from the coast and has the Marin Headlands as a partial buffer on the west. Oaks, madrones, laurels, and other hardwoods grow on the leeward side of the island, which is the only place along the trails described in this section that you will find native woodlands.

When to Go and What to Take

Save your hike on the Marin Headlands or down into Rodeo Valley for a day when the winds have let up. On an overcast day in summer, you will have to dress warmly even if the wind is not strong. On a hot, sunny day, you will want a slight breeze for the walk along Wolfback Ridge or up to the top of Mount Livermore on Angel Island. During the cooler days of summer, when the fog is creeping through the Golden Gate and curling over the highest summits on the Marin Headlands, you will often be able to find a warm spot—even a warm beach—on the northeast side of Angel Island. The beaches should all be saved for the warm weather, at least if you plan to don a swimsuit. Except for those on the leeward side of Angel Island, the beaches in this area are largely exposed to the fog and offshore winds. Nevertheless, suitable days for sunbathing occur during all seasons of the year. Hikers, of course, can withstand much cooler weather, so long as they are dressed warmly. The key to choosing a successful hike near the Golden Gate is to be aware that the weather is highly changeable and that small changes in terrain can make big differences in wind, fog, and temperature. Except during the most inclement weather, you should be able to select a comfortable hike from among those described here.

You will need to carry water if you plan a long hike in the area. It is available only at Baker's Beach, Kirby Cove, and Ayala Cove on Angel Island. On exposed slopes, such as those on the Marin Headlands and Wolfback Ridge, sunglasses and a hat will be useful. Heavy-soled boots are not necessary for any of the walks, but your hiking shoes should be sturdy and comfortable. Bare feet, of course, are *de rigeur* for the beaches. Dogs are prohibited on all the beaches and trails within the Golden Gate National Recreation Area. Horseback riding is permitted in the Marin Headlands and adjacent hills and valleys. Cyclists will find both the old dirt roads on the headlands and Angel Island good places to ride. Bus service is available to points at or near all but one of the trailheads described in this section.

The GGNRA

All the hikes in this section are within the boundaries of the Golden Gate National Recreation Area, known locally—

and not without some humor—as the GGNRA. Formed by an Act of Congress and signed into law on October 27, 1972, this magnificent addition to the National Park System is the largest urban park in the nation, comprising about 34,000 acres of land and offshore water in San Francisco and western Marin County. Its border on the west is the Point Reyes National Seashore, and Samuel P. Taylor State Park on the east. It includes Mount Tamalpais State Park, Muir Woods National Monument, Angel Island State Park, and Marin Headlands State Park. These units are managed separately but in accordance with the goals and programs of the GGNRA. Many areas within the GGNRA are still privately owned or continue to be used by the military; consult the Park Service before attempting to walk in these areas.

GGNRA headquarters are located at Fort Mason in San Francisco, which you can reach by driving north on Van Ness Avenue and turning left on Bay Street; Fort Mason is on your right. The National Park Service also maintains a visitor center in the Marin Headlands at Rodeo Lagoon. To reach the center, drive north on U.S. 101 to the Alexander Avenue exit, just after crossing the Golden Gate Bridge. In a quarter mile, turn left on a paved road leading to a narrow tunnel through the ridge. Wait for the signal to turn green before proceeding through this one-lane tunnel. On the other side, follow the paved road to the lagoon. Cross between two sections of the lagoon to the opposite shore and keep left at the fork. Follow the road to the parking lot at Cronkhite Beach. The visitor center is on the north side of the parking lot.

The best trail map to the GGNRA is the "Recreational Map, Golden Gate National Recreation Area," published by C. E. Erickson and Associates. It is available at park headquarters, the Marin Headlands visitor center, and at hiking equipment outlets throughout the Bay Area. The map shows which property remains reserved by the military, which is private, and which is open to hikers. Since the publication of this map the property along Wolfback Ridge and in the Rodeo Valley has been purchased by the National Park Service and is now open to hikers. The map will continue to become obsolete in this fashion as other private parcels are bought up.

That the GGNRA actually exists seems a miracle; in fact, it is the fruit of hard labor by many dedicated conservationists in the Bay Area. It is a tribute to the people of the region and to their representatives in Congress. They have left all of us the most magnificent and extensive metropolitan park in the world. Together, the GGNRA, Point Reyes National Seashore, Samuel P. Taylor State Park, and the watershed lands of the Marin Municipal Water District total more than 100,000 acres of land open to hikers, horsemen, picnickers, sunbathers, birdwatchers, and naturalists.

1. BAKER'S BEACH

Baker's Beach is the most protected beach in San Francisco, thanks to a backdrop of cypress and pines, which shelter secluded picnic tables and benches that face both the Golden Gate and the Pacific. Yet even here, when a northwest wind is blowing and the fog is moving through the narrow strait, the chill can be discouraging. So, for this walk, choose a time when the air is calm and the sun bright—unless, of course, you relish the solitude and exhilaration that are the sure rewards of a gray, windy day. Bare feet and bathing suits are luxuries of warm weather; otherwise, tennis shoes and a warm jacket are advisable. You may want to bring binoculars to view sea birds and the distant Marin Headlands.

From San Francisco, drive toward the Golden Gate Bridge and take the last exit—signed "Golden Gate Bridge Viewing Area and Presidio Exit"—just before you reach the toll plaza. After proceeding through the underpass, you may leave your car in any of several parking areas. The San Francisco Municipal Railway provides bus service to Baker's Beach. For precise routes and scheduling, call 673-3864. If you wish to begin your walk from the north end of the beach, nearest the bridge, drive past the concrete bunkers, which once hid the guns that guarded the Golden Gate, and turn right (before you reach Lincoln Blvd.) into Langdon Court. This leads around the military storage areas into an unexpected parking lot overlooking the bridge. From here, you can walk all the way to Baker's Beach, staying high in the forested area as long as you like before cutting down to the beach. If you wish to begin your hike from the south end of the beach, continue past Langdon

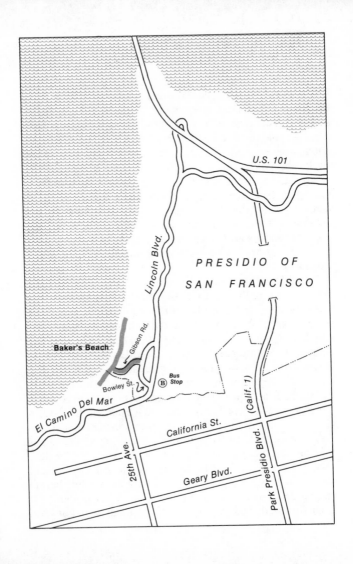

Court to Lincoln Blvd. and down Lincoln to Bowley Street, where the Park Service has provided parking places, picnic tables, and bathrooms.

Baker's Beach used to be a kind of private "word-of-mouth" beach, shared by the army personnel of the nearby Presidio with those lucky San Franciscans who had discovered the winding dirt road (now paved) called Bowley Street. Now, the beach and the cliffs on which you walk are part of the Golden Gate National Recreation Area. Like the Marin Headlands across the Golden Gate, they were inadvertently preserved from development by the U.S. Army, which long ago fortified both sides of the strait in defense of both city and harbor. We can be thankful for their occupation; otherwise this beautiful parklike area, surely among the most valuable real estate in San Francisco, would long ago have succumbed to town houses or apartment buildings.

Back in 1870, the army also began to plant the trees you see all around you, which would make these trees about the same age as those in Golden Gate Park. One might wish they had not been planted in such orderly rows, but it is enough that they prospered, eventually forming the great gothic arches of open forest you can see as you walk along this rim over Baker's Beach.

When all this land belonged to the King of Spain, back in the 1700s, it was a desolate, windswept spot, valued primarily for defense. According to English explorer George Vancouver, who made several voyages into the bay in the late eighteenth and early nineteenth centuries and was the first Englishman to describe Spain's dying outpost on the north Pacific, the Spanish, using Indian labor, had constructed a "square area whose sides were about 200 yards in length enclosed by a mud wall. . . . Above this wall the thatched roofs of their low small houses just made their appearance . . . the windows were holes without glass." All that is left of this adobe fortification is a legend to the effect that its walls are buried beneath the officer's club at the Presidio.

The army planted this bleak headland with Monterey pine (*Pinus radiàta*) and Monterey cypress (*Cupressus macrocarpa*). The pines are the taller trees and can be distinguished from other pines by their thick, dark green foliage, with the needles growing in clusters of three; their dark, blackish bark; and the closed cones that grow along the limbs. This pine is endemic to certain places farther south along the coast and to three of the offshore islands of southern California. It is considered by botanists to be an ancient species whose heyday has passed insofar as its natural range is concerned. Ironically, because it is perhaps the fastest growing pine in the world, and among the most beautiful, this tree has been planted extensively in parks and gardens all over the globe.

The Monterey cypress has an even more restricted range than the Monterey pine, growing only on the exposed headlands overlooking Carmel Bay. Instead of needles, the cypress has aromatic, scale-like branchlets. The cones are knobby, one-inch balls, green when young, but later turning a deep shiny brown. You find the cones on the ground in their old age, opened up to let the tiny brown seeds out. Some of the cypresses grow tall and straight; others lie close to the ground, almost creeping up the dunes.

The National Park Service has put picnic tables among these trees for those who prefer to enjoy their lunches in seclusion and out of the wind. Where a particularly beautiful wind-twisted pine or cypress provides the frame, you may discover a picnic table with a breathtaking view of the Marin Headlands across the strait. As you get closer to the beach, you will find small groups of tables with charcoal grills, but no water. The Park Service is clearing away all the dead limbs of the last hundred years, thereby giving the whole area a charming, open quality, so that you are never quite out of sight or sound of the sea.

When you decide to leave the trees and walk down the footpaths to the beach, you find yourself in another whole plant world. Here, the army has stabilized the dunes with the familiar "ice plant"—you will easily recognize its fleshy stems and bright pink or yellow flowers. Although imported from South America and used widely in landscaping, ice plants have escaped into the wild along the coast, becoming naturalized in many areas. The species with the yellow flowers is known as the Hottentot fig (*Mesembryanthemum edule*), and that with the pink flowers as the sea fig (*Mesembryanthemum chilense*). Misnamed in more ways than one, these plants are not related to figs but are members of the carpetweed family, which includes New Zealand spinach, another familiar garden plant that has escaped into the wild. You will find it here as well among the other beach plants. Its leaves are good either cooked or raw.

There are also native plants to be found on this walk. On your way down to the sand, look for beach sagewort (*Artemisia pycnocephala*), a relative of the coast sagebrush. Ranging along the coast from Monterey County to southern Oregon, it is easily recognized by its woolly, silver-gray leaves. It grows about one to two feet high. You will also find dune lupine (*Lupinus chamissonis*) lining the path. It is easy to identify in spring, when it bears abundant spikes of fragrant purple flowers. At other times of the year look for its distinctive palmate compound leaves, with each narrow leaflet radiating from a single center like the rays of a star. As you get closer to the beach, you will notice that the various plants tend to get progressively smaller, some having very delicate, sprawling shapes.

Just offshore is Helmet Rock, a favorite resting place for cormorants, which may sit there holding their wings out to dry in the sun. They are diving birds, and the mainstay of their diet is fish, but unlike ducks, cormorants lack oil glands to keep their feathers dry. So they must hang their wings out to dry like so much laundry, a comical posture that belies their grace in the water. There are three species of cormorant along the California coast, and you will need binoculars to tell two of them apart. The pelagic cormorant, in spring at least, is easily recognized by its prominent white flank patches; the double-crested cormorant and Baird's cormorant are more difficult to tell apart. Notice the color of their rather small throat patches: the double-crested's is dull orange, the Baird's deep blue.

Baker's Beach is one mile long and, depending on the tide, about fifty feet wide. As at Point Reyes, the tide here can be very high and the surf rough, completely covering the beach and breaking at the base of the cliffs. Do not wander too far along the beach if you are not sure whether the tide is coming in or going out. There are parking places at the end of Bowley Drive. Nearby, among pines, cypresses, and eucalyptus are several especially attractive picnic areas. The beach itself is remarkably clean and a pleasure to walk on, rest on, or sculpt into castles.

You might like to sit at one of the sheltered tables and drink in the view—towering above you, the immense orange bridge, and across the water, the steep, wild cliffs of the Marin Headlands, which, like this beach, are part of the Golden Gate National Recreation Area. In summer and fall they look forbidding and sere, but hike them in winter or spring, after the rains have done their work, and you will find them bright with wildflowers and alive with birds. On the west the headlands culminate in Point Bonita, site of a Coast Guard light that is closed to the public.

Beneath the Golden Gate, buried in the deep silt washed down from the Sacramento and San Joaquin rivers, are wrecks that would-be treasure hunters would like to explore. But here the sea has claimed the booty, whether English sterling, Spanish gold, or bullion from the gold rush. The buried hulks are no more, having been tossed and smashed by the same tides that have confounded every sailor making his first attempt to tack in or out of the Golden Gate.

In heading back to your car, you can follow your mood and the weather. It is possible to walk back the entire distance through the trees on the upward part of the cliffs, sometimes bearing closer to Lincoln Avenue. Or if you prefer, you may cut diagonally through the woods and beach flowers to the even higher woods in the direction of the Golden Gate Bridge. Finally, you may walk back along the beach itself, so long as you head up to high ground at the point where you meet the sign reading: "Hazardous Area Due to High Tides."

Having come to Baker's Beach once, you are sure to return—for the views, the history, the charm of a lonely beach, or for a quiet walk on a small wild fringe of San Francisco. It is part of the contagious charm of this city, indeed of the entire Bay Area, that places such as Baker's Beach have withstood the ravages of time and clever men.

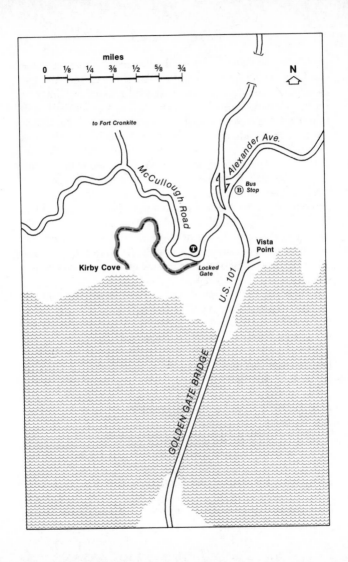

2. KIRBY COVE

Two of the best picnic tables in the Bay Area sit on a little bluff at Kirby Cove. They offer a most elegant view of the Golden Gate, and you can enjoy it from a sunny, wind-free spot tucked into the steep cliffs of the Marin Headlands. From the cove you look directly across the water to the Sea Cliff district of San Francisco. On your left is the bridge and beyond, the downtown district. On your right, the open Pacific stretches out from Land's End. The entire scene is framed by cypress trees. Kirby Cove is an ideal destination for family outings and makes a pleasant, easy walk for a bright afternoon.

Once you have arrived, there are plenty of things for everyone to do. For the children, the old abandoned army fortifications will provide hours of amusement. Adults can either relax on the beach or take out their field guides and study the birds and plants of the area. Sea birds wheel overhead and pass back and forth over the water. For a hundred years or so, nothing but deer have browsed the coastal scrub on the headlands, and as a result they are ablaze with wildflowers from March through May. After winter rains, mushroom fanciers can have a field day. In January you may find twenty or more species of fungus under the trees, ranging from the deadly *Amanita pantherina* pushing its yellow cap with white warts up through the eucalyptus leaves, to hundreds of ashy coral fungus, growing like white asparagus fingers under the cypress trees.

Whatever you do, remember that Kirby Cove is not a good place to swim. A look at the topographic map for the area will show a steep drop-off just beyond the rock offshore from the cove. This, combined with a swift running tide through the Golden Gate, makes swimming safe only for experts. Occasionally, members of the Dolphin Club, in San Francisco, will swim from the city to Kirby Cove, a distance of five miles. But for most people, splashing in the waves is about all that is safe to attempt.

From San Francisco, cross the Golden Gate Bridge to the Alexander Avenue offramp, just past the Vista Point exit. Almost immediately, turn left and drive under the freeway. At the fork, keep right, driving up into the hills through an open gate. Not far beyond, you will see a road branch off downhill on your left. It is barred by a locked gate and is posted with a sign reading, "Kirby Cove State Park— Group Reservations Only." The sign refers to camping, which is available only to organized groups. Hikers are welcome anytime. You can park on the wide gravel shoulders on either side of the road. You can also take a Golden Gate Transit Authority bus to Alexander Avenue and walk up the road to the Kirby Cove trailhead, which will add about a half-mile each way to the hike. Take the 4, 10, or 20 (Sausalito) buses from the East Bay Terminal, at Fremont and Mission in San Francisco. For other stops in the city, and for exact schedules, call 332-6600. From here, it is about a mile down to the cove, and a fairly steep walk back up, though an easy enough one for most people. Carry as little as you can, although you may not be able to resist field guides, binoculars, and a hand lens for examining plants. There are picnic tables, charcoal grills, running water, and latrines at the beach.

Once you have parked your car, go past the gate and head downhill on the road. The sweet fragrance riding on the breeze is likely to be from the low-growing coast sage-

, and flecks of mica. Down at the end of the
e bridge, several fisherman may be perched
the rocks, casting into the sea. Each year a
o captures a fisherman from these or other
nd the Bay Area.

e is running out it is possible to make a dash
s at the beach end of the cove. You can stand
llow rocks and listen to the deafening roar of
is amplified by the caves. The movement of
ing and bending these rocks, is never more
the caves, where the layers have been rolled
ght, like giant roller coasters. It is a crazy,
ture that suits the mood of the sea.

idepool life to observe here—the surf is too
drop-off too steep. Only occasionally is a
washed up on the shore. There are some
e rocks, but even the cliffs that catch the
id of algae. On the offshore rock, cormor-
ately, sometimes all facing in the same
gulls, of course, squabble endlessly.

ost fun here is watching the boats in the bay
hat come and go from all over the world.
ats toss up and down in small armadas, the
avenger gulls flying above their wakes.
smartly into the breeze under the bridge and
the tides running so strong that even though
e moving at a good pace they don't get far,
ack by the force of the tide. On the other
ing ships coming in with the tide move so
re gone almost before you can make out the
as they secure the ship for its arrival in
n Francisco.

brush (*Artemisia californica*). Not a true sage of the salvia
family, this silvery-green shrub with the feathery leaves
(which are fun to pinch and sniff) is related to the sagebrush
that covers the desert expanses of the Great Basin. If the
wind is blowing hard up on top, rest assured that once you
are around the first big bend in the road it will die down, not
to be felt again until you come back up. The walk down is a
good time to dawdle, enjoying not only the superb view of
the bay, but also the eye-level gardens on the rocky cliff
above the road.

By mid-January, the water from the winter rains is
seeping down over hundreds of layers of red sandstone. Dirt

has washed down to fill in the small ledges. The rock itself is fairly soft and splits off at the touch. Its layers are bent and thrust up at sharp angles. Along the various strata and cracks, plants have won footholds and grow in small hanging gardens. Under the hand lens, mosses take on surprisingly different aspects. One grows like a thick mat with long furry feelers that overlap three to four inches, appearing only under other plants, where it thrives in the damp shade. In more open places, another moss grows in rosettes, the newest growth being shaped like small, bright yellow-green stars. From the clusters rise delicate hairs, not over a quarter of an inch long, with tiny capsules on the tips that move as the water drips through them. Each capsule holds spores, which in turn germinate to form the gametophytes from which both male and female mosses start their new generations. The life cycle of ferns is similar.

Mixed in the moss gardens are lichens, of which the pixie cups are easiest to identify, as they are shaped like small goblets. They form irregular patches of silver-gray crust on the rock, each being a colony of thousands of individual lichens. Perfectly symmetrical, they look like microscopic versions of the dried exoskeletal case of the purple sea urchin.

If you come here in winter, you may notice under the Douglas firs hundreds of ashy coral fungus, looking like pale coral fingers pushing up through the needles. If you enjoy looking for mushrooms, Kirby Cove will delight you. But remember that gathering mushrooms for eating is a risky business for everyone but experts—and even they can be fooled. Edible and poisonous species may sometimes look very much alike, and there is no sure test by which many species can be safely separated in the field. Seeing a

3. MARIN HEADLANDS

It is possible to stand on a hilltop covered with wildflowers and look down on the top of the north tower of the Golden Gate Bridge, only to look up moments later and see an osprey hanging almost motionless overhead. The ridge crest of the Marin Headlands is no fearful height, but a splended perch from which to view the bay on one side and the ocean on the other. The headlands rise steeply from the water, but their tops are rounded and grassy. Now part of the Golden Gate National Recreation Area, the fifteen square miles of rolling hills, steep cliffs, hidden beaches, and lagoons were until recently the property of the U.S. Army, which occupied the site in an effort to guard the entrance of the great bay from attack. It is the wonderful serendipity of history that these precious headlands thereby should have been kept in trust, safe from the development that swarmed over most of the other hills in the Bay Area, to become meadows in the sky for viewing San Francisco and the Golden Gate.

The top of almost every hill has an abandoned concrete lookout erected years ago by the military. The hills themselves are tunneled with storage caves. Loops of barbed wire have dropped, rusted and broken, into the grass in places. Dirt roads, some of them really more like extended ruts, lead to the old installations. For the hiker these raods can be useful, especially on the leeward side of the hills, where the coastal scrub is so thick as to be impenetrable—a combination of coyote bush, poison oak, cucumber vine, cow parsnip, poison hemlock, and huckleberry. Where there are springs or seeps, the scrub may be five feet high; in drier spots, three feet is more typical. In either case, what

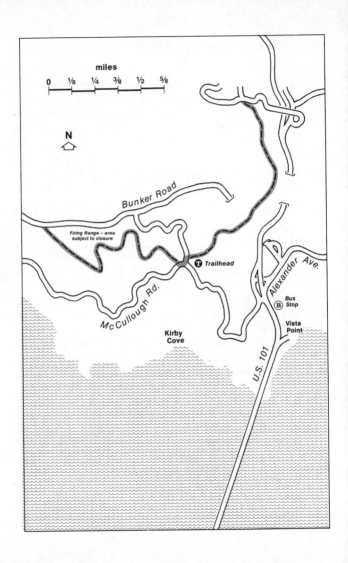

appear at first to be trails often turn out to be impassable deer tracks.

Getting around is much easier on the grassy hilltops. Here, people have made footpaths that connect each ridge top with the next, or else lead up to the best views and down again. Exposed to the strong winds that blow through the Golden Gate, the scrub, where it exists at all, is sparse and low. Great curious rocks are perched about the hilltops, so weathered and covered with lichen that their original color can only be seen when they shed a thin layer of old rock after the winter rains.

Because the headlands are largely open country, you can park almost anywhere and strike out for the top of the nearest hill to get your bearings, and then continue from there, eventually dropping down to a paved or graded dirt road to wind back to your car. But one of the best places to start your walk is a three-way junction about three-quarters of a mile past the road leading down to Kirby Cove. From San Francisco, drive across the Golden Gate Bridge to the Alexander Avenue turn-off. Go left under the freeway and keep left where the road forks, winding up the hill and passing beyond a wire fence. Continue past the road leading down to Kirby Cove until you arrive at the intersection. You can also take a Golden Gate Transit Authority bus to Alexander Avenue and walk up the road to the parking area at the intersection, which will add about a mile each way to your hike. Take the 4, 10, or 20 (Sausalito) bus from the East Bay Terminal, at Fremont and Mission in San Francisco. For other stops in the city, and for exact scheduling, call 332-6600.

Here you can pull off the road in a protected spot. The paved road to your left is now controlled by the army and is occasionally closed for weekend training, when there is "impact firing" going on at Fort Barry below. When the gate on this road is open it is safe to proceed. The grassy hill to the north has an obvious footpath to the top, where it connects to a dirt road and still another trail, which heads north toward Marin City.

This hilltop is a favorite place for observing hawks and vultures, particularly in the fall, when the passage of migrating hawks overhead, including species seen only occasionally in this area, can be spectacular. The headlands are, in general, a paradise for birds—and bird watchers. In the winter months, Rodeo Lagoon, which is visible from the top of this hill, is aswarm with wintering ducks and shorebirds. Herons and egrets of four species are common there most of the year. The rocks off nearby Cronkhite Beach are good places to look for gulls, pelicans, and cormorants. During the fall the entire headlands serve as a landfall for migrating songbirds, including a number of rare eastern warblers that for reasons not entirely understood have strayed from their accustomed migratory routes. The headlands are renowned among Bay Area birders for their impressive yield of rare species.

From the hilltop, the footpath in the grass becomes a dirt road moving from hill to hill. On your right San Francisco Bay spreads out before you, its blue surface dotted with white sailboats puffing out their spinnaker sails as they pick up the breeze. On your left is the first of a series of lovely valleys that grace the headlands. In the distance is the ocean. Directly below on your left is the army resident housing and rifle range. You are walking along an 800-foot ridge that parallels U.S. 101 below. You can walk for about a mile on this dirt road until you reach a power-line tower and the beginning of Wolfback Ridge, where you come to locked gates.

At the locked gates, pick up a trail leading down on your left. This deer track clings to the steep hillside and shows signs of having been used by an occasional hiker. Although the grass is slippery and the footing tricky at times, it is possible for a reasonably agile person to make his way another mile along this elusive path until he reaches the junction of Wolfback Ridge Road and Ridge Road. Directly ahead is a dirt road winding up to a radar station. To the left is a gravel and dirt road that loops about four miles to the ocean. If you want to walk to Sausalito, slip through the barbed-wire fence on your right, which has been cut away in many places, and walk a short way down Wolfback Ridge Road to the U.S. 101 overpass. After crossing over the freeway, descend a flight of wooden steps to the firehouse at the Spencer Avenue cut-off, from where you can follow a pleasant winding road into the heart of Sausalito.

If this is more of a hike than you want to attempt, turn back on the ridge top whenever you like and retrace your steps toward the south. As you head down to your car you can see that a paved road winds around and up by the ocean and a gravel road follows the leeward side of the same hills. Take either one. The paved road by the sea connects to several dirt roads that drop fairly steeply down to the leeward road above the rifle range. Grassy paths along the way lead up to vantage points, and here and there flattened spots in the grass mark recent picnics.

If you spread a picnic in the headlands, watch out for both ticks and poison oak. Ticks look like miniature crabs, and once one digs into the skin, removing it without leaving the head inside is difficult. Poison oak (*Rhus diversiflora*) thrives on the headlands. In the wetter places it may form a three-foot barrier of shrubs. In other places it forms a vine, which grows up among other, more innocent plants. In any season but winter you can identify it by its oaklike leaves, which usually grow in groups of three. In spring and summer mature foliage is brilliant green, turning bright red after the first cold weather of autumn. The leaves drop in winter. If they happen to touch poison oak, most people break out in blisters, which itch and spread. Some people seem susceptible even to the plant's air-borne pollen, still others are virtually immune. Deer eat it and bees gather its honey, but humans should avoid it. Early Californians devised various balms and ointments for treating poison oak blisters; one used by the Indians was a paste made from soap plant or amole (*Chlorogalum pomeridianum*), a member of the lily family found all over the headlands. But rather than dig up the hillsides looking for amole, wash the skin as soon as possible with cold water and a strong soap. Consult a physician if the outbreak becomes severe. Neither poison oak nor ticks should discourage you from exploring the headlands, though; both can be avoided easily with a little care.

The green, stubby shrub you see all over the hills is the coyote bush or chaparral broom (*Baccharis pilularis consanguinea*), which sometimes is bent flat by the wind and other times grows waist high. The Latin name means "many hairlike berries living together." One common name, "fuzzy-wuzzy," comes from the tufts of fluff that cover the plant at certain seasons. The leaves are saw-toothed and mildly abrasive to the touch. Almost as common as the coyote bush is coast sagebrush (*Artemisia californica*), which is delightful for its soft silvery-green foliage and fresh, pungent aroma.

On a warm day a wave of herbal perfume rolls across the headlands, the fragrances of sagebrush, yarrow, and cow parsnip mixed with the smell of the sea. Yarrow (*Achillea borealis*) resembles Queen Anne's lace of the East Coast and has a spicy smell. Its green fuzzy leaves are so pungent they will make your eyes water, but the lacy white flower is mild enough to enjoy. Cow parsnip, an outsized member of the parsley family, is easily recognized by its big, coarse, white, umbrella-shaped flowers and its gigantic maple-shaped leaves. If you take too close a whiff of the flower, it will clear up your sinuses, but from a distance, diluted with salt air and the softer perfumes of sagebrush and yarrow, its pungency is a welcome treat.

Among the native plants on the headlands are several invasive European imports, which, however undesirable, are here to stay. Two of them are particularly interesting for their literary associations. One, poison hemlock (*Corium maculatum*), is related to the cow parsnip, and it is famous for having been the source of the deadly infusion that Socrates drank in prison. Poison hemlock has beautiful lacy leaves, but one whiff of its bitter essence is ample warning that this is one plant to avoid. The second famous European plant that grows commonly on the headlands is the scarlet pimpernel (*Anagallis arvensis*), which is actually salmon-orange. The tiny flowers have wet purple centers with gleaming golden anthers and stigma.

If you do not witness the whale migration, you will still not be at a loss for things to watch on the waters far below. There is always something going on at the entrance to San Francisco Bay. Fishing boats are scattered like insects on a pond, marked frequently by circling gulls anxious to snatch a part of the catch. The water runs up to six knots beneath the Golden Gate as the tide carries silt from the Sacramento/San Joaquin delta to the sea. The fast-moving tide of San Francisco Bay has always been both a curse and a blessing to sailors, who must go with the tides rather than fight them. Early mariners learned that they could not enter the bay against the swift tide, but had to wait until it turned.

From the top of the ridge that faces the ocean you may follow the road south along the crest and then drop down to the parking area. Or you may turn north and wind down toward Point Bonita. The road drops down to Rodeo Lagoon. Circling back, about a half mile south of the lagoon, past the rifle range, you come to a paved road that leads up past an abandoned quarry. This road winds uphill for a mile back to the parking lot and the beginning of your hike. You cannot really get lost in this part of the headlands because you can always locate the ocean, the bay, or the lagoon, and then head back to where you started.

Distances, however, are deceptive in these open grass-lands. As in the desert or at sea, you can see distant landmarks long before you reach them. The old army roads are generally well graded and easy to walk on. No drinking water is available except at the firehouse near Rodeo Lagoon, so carry your own. Do not drink from the seeps or springs you may encounter on the way.

Seen from a distance, the headlands look monotonous. Only up close does their variety become evident. Even as you walk over them, there seem to be few living creatures besides birds, yet with patience and luck you may see the waving tail of a skunk making its way through the grass-lands or startle a gray fox as he sniffs the breeze.

4. RODEO VALLEY

This walk visits a little-known valley tucked behind the Marin Headlands and just a few minutes west of the busy tourist haunts of Sausalito. It is an easy ramble through bright, open country where shade is scarce, but where the heat of the afternoon is usually tempered by ocean breezes. The halfway point on this five-mile loop is a stand of cypress and eucalyptus trees beside the remains of the old Silva Ranch. These trees are the only ones in the valley, and this rare patch of shade is the obvious first choice for a picnic lunch. Be sure to carry your own water, for none fit to drink is available along the way. Although there are a few stretches on the way down to the valley where the trail is faint and the slope fairly steep, you will not need heavy-soled boots for this hike; good walking shoes will be perfect. Since the entire loop takes only about three hours, you can do it either in a morning or afternoon. During the winter you will probably want a windbreaker even on sunny days, likewise on foggy summer days. For the best wildflower display, take the walk in late spring or early summer. For bird watchers, April and October are probably the best months. If you just like to walk, anytime of the year is good.

From San Francisco drive north across the Golden Gate Bridge. After leaving the Waldo Tunnel, get in the right-hand lane and take the next—Spencer Avenue—exit. Right after getting off the freeway, you will come to a sign pointing ahead to Monte Mar Drive and right to Spencer Avenue. Just beyond the sign is a fire station and a dirt parking area adjacent to the frontage road. Park in this lot and climb the stairs across the street from the fire house.

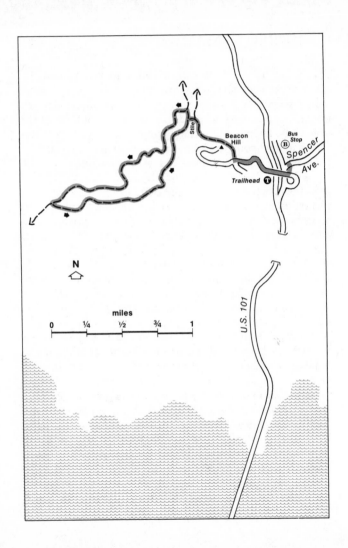

You can also take a Golden Gate Transit Authority bus to Spencer Avenue. Take the 70 or 80 (Santa Rosa) buses, or the 50 (Novato) bus, from the East Bay Terminal, at Fremont and Mission in San Francisco. For other stops in the city, and for exact schedules, call 332-6600. Turn right at the top of the stairs and cross the freeway overpass. Continue straight ahead up the paved road. Despite the "private road" signs along the way, hikers are welcome here. The road winds uphill for about a quarter mile to the crest of Wolf Ridge and a four-way junction. If you wish to climb Beacon Hill for a 360-degree panorama of the Bay Area, keep straight ahead. You can easily make this side trip and still have plenty of time for the Rodeo Valley loop. If you wish to save Beacon Hill for another day, turn right at the junction on the dirt track amusingly misnamed Alta "Avenue." It leads uphill through a splendid eucalyptus grove that will provide the only shade on this hike until you reach the trees at the old Silva Ranch in the bottom of the valley. After leaving the grove, the track swings to the left on an open grassy ridge. To your left is Beacon Hill and its cluster of radio antennas, to the right a couple of rocky knolls crowned with windblown shrubs. To the north the skyline is dominated by the long, impressive ridge of Mount Tamalpais. As you move away from the trees and past the first knoll, you can look down on Richardson Bay, which is separated from the larger San Pablo Bay to the east by the Tiburon Peninsula. On a clear day you can see the hills of Sonoma, Napa, and Solano counties in the distance, about twenty-five miles away.

Once past the knolls, the road begins to drop slightly, though it stays on the ridge crest. On the left a dense growth of coastal scrub sweeps uphill toward the antennas. On the right grasslands lead toward the brink of the ridge. If you are tempted to ramble through the grass here, be aware that there are rattlesnakes on this ridge. The chances of meeting one are slight, but you should proceed with some caution and enough noise to give any snakes in the vicinity ample warning of your approach.

As the brushy slopes of Beacon Hill give way on your left to an expanding view of Rodeo Valley, you will see a hiker's stile surmounting the barbed wire fence along the road. Cross this stile to a second road just below the one you have been walking on until now. From the stile you can see the entire Rodeo Valley, which is a broad cul-de-sac extending east from the ocean. The high, rolling ridge to the south overlooks the Golden Gate beyond (see Section 3). To the west, at the far end of the Rodeo Valley, you can see a corner of Rodeo Lagoon, which is cut off from the ocean by the sands of Cronkhite Beach. This hike does not go all the way to the lagoon, although this is certainly possible if you have arranged a car shuttle. You are on the crest of Wolf Ridge, which climbs to the west.

Those who do wish to walk the entire route should turn right on the road just beyond the stile. This is the *Wolf Trail*. Your return route will be the left fork of this road, which you can see making a long, easy traverse of the west flank of Beacon Hill across the way. Far below in the valley, you can see the isolated grove of trees that marks the point where you pick up the road back. From this point on, dogs are prohibited on the trail.

The road on the right drops to a saddle from which you get excellent views of Richardson Bay to the north, with San Pablo Bay beyond. When the trail begins to climb, look toward the south for expanding views of the north tower of the Golden Gate Bridge, which is just peeping from behind the Marin Headlands; Land's End in San Francisco; and far to the south, San Pedro Point jutting far out into the Pacific. This panorama can be spectacular on a summer day when a low coastal fog is moving through the Golden Gate and the valley below. The ocean itself will resemble a sea of foam probing the continent with long wispy fingers. On such a day you might be perfectly warm on this high sunny ridge yet require a windbreaker once you descend to the fog in the valley below. On other days these hills may be completely enshrouded in a thick gray mist driven inland by strong cold winds; then you should choose another hike.

Just after rounding the shoulder of the ridge, take the old faded track that leaves the road on the left, heading slightly downhill toward some chert outcrops in the grass. (Although the wide dirt road is the clearer, more obvious route, it winds along the ridge top instead of dropping to the valley below.) Just past the outcrops, the old track climbs over a low rise and then makes a long, slightly downhill traverse of the slope. You will come to a path on your left leading to the prominent knoll jutting out from the ridge. This is a fine place to sit awhile, but you should return to the old track if you wish to continue to Rodeo Valley.

During the late spring this trail—this entire walk, in fact—is gaily decked with a wide variety of wildflowers. California poppies splash the grasslands with orange; lupines add shades of blue and lavender; the yellows are provided by the showy wyethia and wild dandelions. Indian paintbrush, of course, adds its dazzling red accent to the display. Other species of wildflowers along this trail include an abundance of pale rose morning glories, blue-eyed grass, buttercups, and checker bloom.

The trail descends gradually to a moist swale, where for the first time on this walk you encounter the beautiful common monkeyflower (*Mimulus guttatus*), which looks like its relative, the garden snapdragon. The monkeyflower's blossoms grow in clusters on long stalks, and they are shaped very much like those of the snapdragon. Both are members of the figwort family, which includes a number of other springtime favorites. The particular variety (*grandis*) of yellow monkeyflower along this trail blooms so abundantly and its flowers are so large that it seems more like a horticultural invention than a native wildflower. Wherever you find it, you can be sure there is water nearby, either at the surface or just below, for the yellow monkeyflower thrives only where moisture is abundant and available year around. In this, it is entirely unlike its close relative the bush monkeyflower (*Mimulus auranticus*), which thrives on hot, dry slopes, and which you will also see along this walk. It is a common member of the coastal scrub and is easily recognized by its salmon-colored flowers.

From the swale the trail bends to the south along the ridge, then drops steeply before giving out altogether. Pick up a faint path through the grass along the left side of a deep erosion gully. In the spring the gully is decorated with California poppies, which redeem this otherwise unpleasant scar. Follow the path downward and toward the left around the hill as you approach a large swale in the valley bottom. Just before you come to a barbed wire fence, cut across the swale on a muddy, but easily recognized track. On the other side, do not follow the track uphill. Instead, look for a faint path leading through the grass on your left. This rounds the knoll and then straightens out along the fence, running through a broad flat grassland. The grove of trees lies directly ahead. On a warm day, this grassland is rich with heady smells. The grass grows up to your knees and has obviously not been grazed for some time. This is a rare spectacle in California, for here, as elsewhere in the country, people seem to assume automatically that if you have a plot of grass you are obliged to put a cow on it.

Presently you will notice an opening in the barbed wire fence on your left. Pass this up to follow the path through a second opening just beyond. The trail swings left toward the trees, dropping down to a small stream before coming to a wide dirt road. This will be your route back up to the ridge. You can see this road all the way up the ridge. On your right are the foundations of the old Silva Ranch and the only shade since the beginning of this hike. This is an excellent place to rest or eat lunch.

To return to the stile, just follow the road toward the right. It makes a long easy traverse of the slope on the south side of the valley. The walk is constantly uphill, but never steep. Your route will be through coastal scrub rather than grasslands, as it was coming down. Wildflowers along this stretch include bush monkeyflower, Indian paintbrush, cow parsnip, yarrow, buttercups, blue-eyed grass, checker bloom, California poppies, lupine, and common monkey-flower. The common shrubs along the trail are ceanothus, poison oak (it has reddish-green or bright green leaves that grow in clusters of three), toyon, coyote bush, and coastal sagebrush. About two-thirds of the way to the top you will come to a resting place in the shade of some tall eucalyptus. From here it is a short uphill walk back to the stile.

5. ANGEL ISLAND

Isolated by water from the cities around it, Angel Island is yet part of the city, historically and physically a short step from San Francisco. It is a city park the likes of which have never been seen before—a true wild place set in the center of a densely populated metropolitan region. Here, you can picnic on the grass, enjoy the spectacular views, lie on uncrowded beaches, study the birds and plants, and hike through woods and grasslands—all within a stone's throw of the capital of Pacific commerce. Indeed, if there is one place where you can truly comprehend the natural wonder of San Francisco Bay, its grand sweep of land, sky, and water, it is from the top of Mount Livermore on Angel Island.

Angel Island is accessible only by boat. Though there are some docking facilities for private craft in Ayala Cove, most visitors arrive via one of the ferries that depart from San Francisco, Berkeley, and Tiburon. Harbor Tours operates ferries from all three cities; McDonough Ferries, from Tiburon only. For precise fares and schedules, call the ferry companies. Do not plan a trip to Angel Island without doing so, for the ferries do not operate every day of the year. The San Francisco ferry terminal is at Fisherman's Wharf, the Berkeley terminal is at the Berkeley Marina at the end of University Avenue, and the Tiburon Terminal is near the shops and restaurants at the end of Tiburon Avenue.

Angel Island is usually warmer than San Francisco and generally free of fog. Ayala Cove, on the north side of the island, is often well protected from the offshore winds that can make other beaches in the Bay Area cold and uncomfortable. The island can vary as much as ten degrees in

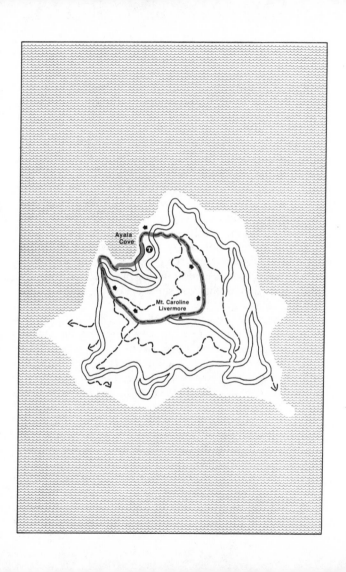

temperature from one side to the other. To find the best weather, ask one of the rangers who live there. Take a picnic and wear your hiking shoes if you plan to do some walking. Carry your own water. You can bring a bike with you. Dogs are not allowed on Angel Island.

Roads and trails loop all around the island, so there are plenty of possible routes to choose from. A trail map is posted on the restrooms near the docks as you get off the ferry; pocket-sized maps are available free at the visitor center, which is located just above the main picnic area. The roads and trails on the islands are all well posted. If the wind isn't blowing, or if you can find a sheltered cove, bring your bathing suit. Ayala Cove is pleasant enough to spend an entire day there, lying on the lawn or walking to one of several overlooks. But the top of Mount Livermore is such a special place that you should make the effort it takes to hike.

There are four ways to get to the top. The *Sunset Trail* is short (one mile) and steep, but by following the switch-backs, instead of cutting across them—as too many people have already done—you should not find the climb too difficult. The last stretch is the steepest, but it is mercifully short. You can also take the *North Ridge Trail* to the top, but the extremely steep climb from Ayala Cove to the crest of the ridge makes it a better choice for your return trip. You can find a third trail by walking west on the macadam road that runs above the park headquarters at Ayala Cove. Follow the road around the western side of the island, passing the side road to West Garrison. A few hundred feet beyond a second side road which leads to Pearls Beach, a trail heads up on your left, joining the Sunset Trail just before the last steep pitch to the top of Mount Livermore. If you would prefer a longer and gentler route to the top, continue on the macadam road past the junction described just above. Pass the rock quarry to a fork; either route is okay, though the left one involves some uphill walking. After the roads rejoin, continue until you come to a crossroads. Turn left on another macadam road. This climbs easily to the top.

From the ferry dock at Ayala Cove, follow the broad dirt walkway that runs along the water to the far end of the picnic grounds. Walk uphill to a road on a narrow boardwalk. Turn right on that road and continue climbing gradually through mixed woods of oak and Monterey pine. Your route turns left when you come to a sign reading "Hazardous Area." Climb up to the paved road, where you get your first panoramic view of Marin County and San Pablo Bay to the north. Directly below you lie Tiburon and Belvedere, and behind them in the distance, the dramatic summit of Mount Tamalpais. To the southwest you can see the Marin Headlands and the Golden Gate Bridge.

Turn right on the paved road. A few feet away is a sign pointing to wooden stairs on the left side of the road. The sign reads: "Sunset Trail to Mount Livermore, 1.0 miles." If you wish to take one of the two alternate routes to the top described previously, ignore the sign and head up the road. If you don't mind walking on macadam, this road can be used to circumnavigate the island. It is ideal, of course, for bicycles. Along the way there are several places to explore, including picturesque West Garrison and beautiful Pearls Beach. The total walk around the island on this road should take you two hours or more, depending on rests and side trips.

From the paved road, the *Sunset Trail* climbs moderately

through oak woodland. The switchbacks on this section are well laid out, but the artificial steps make the trail more difficult than it otherwise might be. The problem with this ingenious stairway is that you have to lift your feet higher on each step than you would on just plain trail. You are climbing up the backbone of a ridge, which becomes obvious once you emerge from the forest into grasslands and coastal scrub. The view from here is an enlarged version of the one below; as you climb, the Bay Area continues to open up before you until, on top of Mount Livermore, the view encompasses a full 360 degrees.

Spring wildflowers in the open grasslands along this ridge include buttercups, California poppies, wyethia—a brilliant yellow native sunflower—brodiaea, checker, and an abundance of blue-eyed grass.

Shortly, you begin switchbacking up a steep section of the ridge crest. At first it might look as if the trail simply ran straight uphill, but this swath is a shortcut across the switchbacks made by hikers in a hurry. The Park Service would like to keep people from cutting across trails because it can eventually lead to serious slope erosion. Besides, the switchbacks make for a far easier climb. At the top of this stretch, you meet a dirt fire road that, like the macadam one below, runs completely around the island. You can pick up one of the alternate routes to Mount Livermore by following this road either left or right, but for the shortest walk cross the road to the wooden stairway and continue switchbacking up the ridge, moving in and out of the oak woodlands with each loop of the trail. On a very hot day these brief stretches of shade are surprisingly welcome and offer good resting places for those tired of the sun. As you move up the ridge, you will notice with envy the shady trees far below at West

Garrison. The beautiful old red brick building was once the quartermaster's warehouse. It is destined to be a museum for the park.

Then, suddenly, San Francisco is spread out before you, a breathtaking view of the city. The best thing about it is that you have earned it. There are no tour buses to this point, no pay telescopes or guard railings. You can see from the skyscrapers of the financial district to the distant pine forests of the Presidio—and pretty much everything in between. Unless you want to rest, resist the temptation to stop here; the top is not far now, and from there the view not just of the city but of the entire Bay Area is grand enough to merit a longer pause.

The trail then climbs the ridge through sagebrush and bracken fern accented with the occasional scarlet of Indian paintbrush. The trail levels out briefly before climbing even more steeply than it has before, this time without switchbacks. Pass the side trail leading off at an acute angle on your right. (This is the trail that takes off from the macadam road just beyond the way down to Pearls Beach.) Haul yourself up this final steep pitch—it's not long—to an old concrete pad with a picnic table. From here the climb is over. Signs point to the actual summit just up the road to your left. (This is the road leading up from the macadam road near Point Blunt. It is the easiest route to the top of Mount Livermore.) Very shortly you will arrive at the broad flat summit, with its old concrete foundations, helicopter pad, and other reminders of when this was a missile site.

From here, the entire Bay Area is spread before you. It is almost too much to take in at one time. To the north, the Richmond-San Rafael Bridge, San Pablo Bay, the distant hills of Napa and Sonoma counties, and on the farthest horizon, the summit of Mount St. Helena, the highest peak in the Bay Area. To the east, Berkeley, Richmond, Oakland, the University of California, the Berkeley-Oakland hills, and Mount Diablo beyond. To the south, San Francisco, the Bay Bridge, Yerba Buena Island and Treasure Island, the south bay, the Santa Cruz mountains to the southwest and Mount Hamilton far to the southeast. To the west, the Golden Gate Bridge, the Marin Headlands, Sausalito, Belvedere, Tiburon, Richardson Bay, and the summit of Mount Tamalpais.

What is it about looking down from a great height that so delights everyone? Is there some peculiar magic involved in picking out from 776 feet what you may be tired of seeing from sea level? Adults as well as children love to distinguish various landmarks from mountain tops. Why? You can ponder this question as you stand on top of Mount Livermore, delighting like everyone else in the power to see, and in having seen, to name.

If it's a sunny day, you may before long want some shade, since you have been in the open most of the way up. At the east end of the flat summit, across the old helicopter pad, you will see a sign marking the *North Ridge Trail*. Follow the trail downhill to the shade of some Monterey pines. Off to your right, through the grass, is perhaps the best place en route for a picnic. Spread yourself out on a gentle grassy slope beneath the pines. Here you will find both sun and shade as well as the dappled fringes where the two meet. The slope drops off steeply. Your luncheon view is a vast sweep from the Berkeley hills to downtown San Francisco, with Alcatraz tossed in to boot. In the spring, you will lie among star lilies and listen to seals barking below.

From the summit, the *North Ridge Trail* descends fairly steeply through open woods thick with wild cucumber and currents to an open grass ridge, from which you can see both the East Bay and Marin County. Notice the different species of pine on your right. This is ponderosa or yellow pine (*Pinus ponderosa*), another transplant on the island. You can distinguish it from the Monterey pine by its longer needles, open cones (the Monterey's generally are closed tight), and more open, lighter-green foliage. The ponderosa pine is native to the montane forests of the West, where it is an abundant and impressive tree.

Continue along the ridge for perhaps a quarter mile before entering oak woods. The grade is easy, and in a short time you leave the woods and can see Ayala Cove below you to the west. From here the trail switchbacks down a heavily eroded, barren slope, which supports only some low madrones and a few manzanitas. The trail continues to drop in very steep switchbacks, coming at last to steps leading down a dirt fire road. A sign for the North Ridge Trail points straight ahead, leading you to another set of steep switchbacks along the edge of the woods. After this long, precipitous descent, you come to a macadam road. Turn right and follow the signed trail leading directly down to Ayala Cove. After crossing an old paved road, you walk down a steep stairway to a few picnic tables on a flat bluff directly overlooking the cove. From here it is a short walk down to your right. Ayala Cove is named for Juan Manuel de Ayala, the first man we know of to captain a ship through the Golden Gate. He entered in August 1775, dropping anchor finally in the protected cove now bearing his name. He called the large island that provided this anchorage "*Isla de Santa Maria de los Angeles*"—Angel Island.

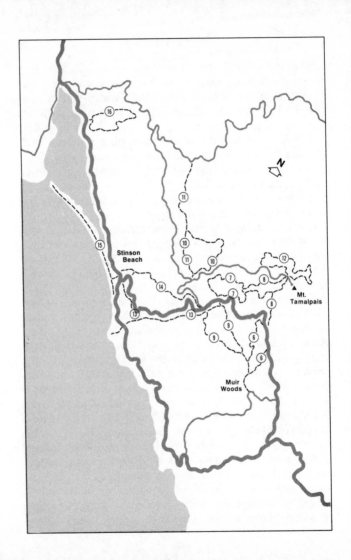

Mount Tamalpais

MOUNT TAMALPAIS (tam'l-PIE-us) or "Mt. Tam," as it is known locally, is the benevolent presiding genius of Marin County and one of the most prominent landmarks of the San Francisco Bay Area. Just ten miles north of San Francisco, its 2,610-foot summit, East Peak, is visible for miles around. Of the prominent peaks in the region, Mt. Tam is the only one directly overlooking the bay. The distance from the water's edge to the summit is less than four and one-half miles. Although its elevation is hardly more than that of many California hills, it has the look and feel of a real mountain, thanks to its precipitous flanks and rocky, pointed summit. The mountain feeling is further accentuated by the dense forests and meadows of its many canyons and the high-country openness of its upper slopes.

The summit of Mt. Tam is really the culmination of a long ridge, which rises abruptly above the Pacific on the west and trends gradually higher toward East Peak, which drops even more abruptly to the edge of San Francisco Bay. Steep canyons intersect both the north and south slopes of the ridge and are drained by fast-flowing streams, which are torrents during the winter but often dry the rest of the year. Some of the streams, however, are spring fed and thus flow all year around.

Mt. Tam is part of the California Coast Range, which consists largely of a series of ridges and valleys trending north-south along the central California coast. The Golden Gate, a few miles south of Mt. Tam, marks the place where the ancient Sacramento River cut a channel through the rising mountain block. The San Francisco Bay is a vast Coast Range valley that was flooded when the oceans began to rise at the end of the last Ice Age. The Coast Range largely consists of ancient marine sediments that were folded and uplifted more than 60 million years ago. In most places, this sedimentary bedrock—known as the Franciscan Formation—is overlain with younger sediments deposited when the older rock still lay beneath the sea. But on Mt. Tam there are no younger sediments, which suggests that this is an ancient highland that has stood above the sea much longer than most of the other hills in the Bay Area. The prominent rock outcrops on Mt. Tam are either serpentine or chert. Serpentine, the state rock of California, is widely associated with the Franciscan sediments, though it is not one of them. It is a green, rather soft rock that looks as if it had been cracked in a thousand places. Chert is the agglutinized remains of billions of tiny marine animals; it can be red, green, or brown. Outcrops of either chert or serpentine tend to support few, if any plants.

The Trails

Mount Tamalpais is an excellent place to hike. Unlike the Marin Headlands, Angel Island, and Point Reyes, which by comparison have been opened to the public only recently, Mt. Tam has been a favorite hiking spot since the last century. As a result it has the finest system of trails of any area around the bay. They are well engineered and well maintained, and though fire roads exist on the mountain, the hiker is seldom forced to depend on them. Dozens of different routes and variations on routes are possible. The hikes in this book should be considered as starting points to help you acquaint yourself with the area. It would have been impossible in a book such as this to describe every trail on Mt. Tam, but when you know the mountain better you will be able to improvise your own hikes. The best trail map to the Mount Tamalpais region is the one published by C. E. Erickson & Associates. It is available at the Pan Toll Ranger Station on Mt. Tam, the Mountain Home fire station, and at hiking equipment outlets throughout the Bay Area. The U.S.G.S. topographical map to Mt. Tam is of little use to hikers.

Most of the trails described in this book begin on or near the Panoramic Highway or its extension to the top of the mountain, the Ridge Crest Road. Two of the hikes begin from the Shoreline Highway—state route 1—near Stinson Beach, and a third from the Fairfax-Bolinas Road on the north side of the mountain. Specific directions to each trailhead are given at the beginning of each hike description. You should also consult a road map of Marin County. Bus service is available every day of the week to Stinson Beach via Mountain Home, Bootjack Camp, and Pan Toll, Stinson Beach, and Audubon Canyon Ranch. Since these are all trailheads, this bus service allows you to leave your car at any one of them and take the bus back from any of the others. For exact schedules, call the Golden Gate Transit District.

Parks and Facilities

Although there are private homes at the base of Mt. Tam on all sides and on the south ridge leading up to Mountain Home, most of the mountain is publicly owned. The peak itself and much of the south and west slopes are included in the 6,200-acre Mount Tamalpais State Park. Picnic facilities are maintained at Bootjack Camp, Pan Toll, Rock Springs, and East Peak. The only campground on the mountain is within the state park at Pan Toll. Since this is a very popular place to camp, advance reservations will probably be necessary. Information and maps are also available from the park headquarters at Pan Toll.

Lying below the state park in a canyon on the south slope of the mountain is the extremely popular Muir Woods National Monument, which was set aside by President Theodore Roosevelt in order to protect the giant redwoods that grow along Redwood Creek. This 520-acre park was donated to the nation by William Kent, an early Bay Area conservationist, and it is visited by hundreds of thousands of tourists every year. In order to protect the redwoods and associated animals and vegetation, no camping or picnicking is allowed within the boundaries of the monument. Hiking is encouraged, however, and there are several fine trails beyond the portion of the park frequented by tourists. The best of these wilder trails are described in this book. Both Muir Woods and Mount Tamalpais State Park are managed as separate units within the Golden Gate National Recreation Area.

Almost all of the north slope of Mt. Tam lies within the 17,000-acre watershed of the Marin Municipal Water District. These lands are open to hikers, and though only three of the walks described in this book are on the watershed lands, examination of the Erickson trail map of Mount Tamalpais will reveal many other possibilities.

There are a few rules for hikers that apply to all the public lands on Mt. Tam. First, dogs, whether leashed or not, are not allowed on the trails. This is not merely for the convenience of other hikers, but for the safety of the wildlife. Dog owners may be skeptical of just how much harm their pets can do to wildlife, but in fact dogs have caused serious problems in many parks around the Bay

Area. Second, do not build fires except in the metal grills especially set aside for this purpose. No fires at all are allowed in Muir Woods National Monument. Third, do not litter the trails; pack out everything you bring in, or where possible, deposit litter in appropriate receptacles. Fourth, do not pollute the streams.

When to Go and What to Take

The best time to hike on Mount Tamalpais is from January through June, when the mountain streams are fullest and the wildflowers are at their best. In addition, this time of the year is blessed with an abundance of bright sunny days that are yet refreshingly cool. Although the flowers diminish along with the streams during the hot, dry months of summer and fall, Mt. Tam remains an excellent place to hike even then. For when summer fogs may have socked in most of the Bay Area, the top of Mt. Tam will often be clear and sunny, and from the upper slopes you will be able to look down on a huge white sea of fog through which poke only the tops of the highest hills in the region. This visual spectacle more than makes up for the scarcity of flowers and water. On the hotter summer days you can find refuge in the mountain's dense redwood forests. The trails through Muir Woods and down Steep Ravine, for example, will be pleasant even when more exposed routes are too warm. The only time to avoid Mount Tamalpais is during a big winter storm, when winds on the mountain can attain hurricane force. Not all storms are so ferocious, but the number of downed trees you see along many of the trails are reminders of what storms up here can be like.

Good walking shoes are perfectly adequate for most of

the trails, though for two or three hiking boots are preferable, and along a few routes they are absolutely necessary. Specific requirements for each trail will be provided in the appropriate descriptions. Other equipment is optional, though amateur naturalists will almost certainly want to carry field guides, binoculars, and hand lenses on most walks. Photographers will find abundant subjects on which to train their lenses.

The Landscape

The outstanding feature of Mount Tamalpais for hikers is the great variety of vegetation and terrain that exists in this rather compact area. In a single day, one can explore redwood forests, mixed hardwood forests, open scrubland, rolling grasslands, rocky stream canyons with cascades and waterfalls, blue lakes, sandy beaches, and salt marsh. As a bonus, most trails offer spectacular views of the surrounding Bay Area, from the rolling hills of west Marin to the concrete towers of San Francisco. On many hikes you can stand at the edge of the forest and see the ocean.

The steep upper slopes of the mountain and the hot lower slopes on the southwest side are largely covered with either chaparral or coastal scrub, miniature forests of sorts that consist almost entirely of shrubby species, with only a smattering of herbaceous and arboreal plants. Scrubland also grows on serpentine soils, which are common on Mt. Tam. The lower, more gradual, and more protected slopes are generally given over to dense forests. In drier areas higher on the mountain, these woodlands will consist of Douglas firs and such hardwood species as tanoak, madrone, laurel, and various oaks. In the moister canyons on both sides of the mountain the predominant forest tree is

the magnificent redwood, which reach
giants of Muir Woods.

Lush grasslands dominate the high r
west slope of the mountain, giving w
moist canyons and to scrublands on t
slopes. In addition, small patches o
called meadows even though they are
sunny islands in the forests. More e
similar to those on most of the hills of
in the lower slopes and adjacent hills o
mountain. These are typical oak
California Coast Range, being more o
than the mixed-evergreen forests high

The north side of the mountain als
reservoirs of the Marin Municipal W
rainy season, when they are full to t
beautiful blue gems set in their b
grassland. But in the dry summer seas
is flowing to the faucets of Marin C
shaved sides become visible, and t
become less attractive, if not actual

On the west Mt. Tam drops abrup
base is the small village of Stinson B
sand over the San Andreas Fault. Stir
offers one of the loveliest white san
Area, and two of the hikes in this boo
Just north of Stinson Beach is Boli
estuary formed where the ocean floo
the Olema Valley. This is a spect
watchers, especially during the winte
Canyon Ranch, where great blue he
nest in the tops of redwood trees.

6. MUIR WOODS VIA FERN CREEK TRAIL

Muir Woods National Monument, situated in a protective canyon on the southern slopes of Mount Tamalpais, preserves the last stand of primeval redwood forest within easy reach of San Francisco. The next closest major groves are more than an hour's drive from the city and require an entire day for a proper excursion. But for Muir Woods, most Bay Area residents need only a crisp morning or bright afternoon.

Unfortunately, most visitors see only the one-mile stretch of trail that winds through the great trees beside Redwood Creek, near the park headquarters. If they were to walk farther, they would discover several delightful trails to choose from—an old wagon road, the abandoned grade of the Mount Tamalpais and Muir Woods Railroad, a footpath along Fern Canyon Creek, the giant serpentine stairway up to Bootjack Camp, the long easy ascent up the *Ben Johnson Trail* to Pan Toll, and the *Ocean View Trail* up to Mountain Home. This network of trails permits many loop trips from Panoramic Highway down into Muir Woods and back again. So if you want to best experience the quiet beauty of Muir Woods, do not follow the crowd to the park entrance, but begin higher on the mountain, taking one of the back trails leading down from Pan Toll, Bootjack Camp, or Mountain Home.

Although redwoods are splendid almost any time of day or year, the thin shafts of light that filter down to the forest floor on a bright afternoon in midwinter make this an especially beautiful time to visit Muir Woods. Even rainy days can be pleasant so long as you keep your feet dry, for

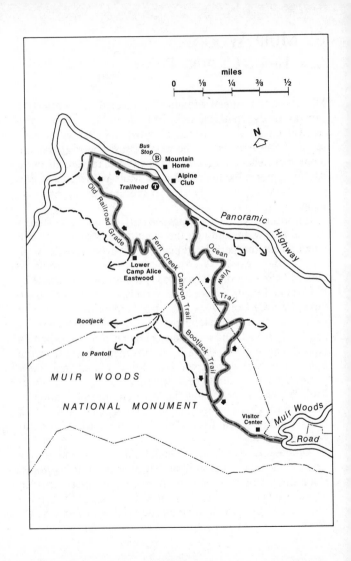

the redwood forest's dense canopy keeps out much of the rain. Then, it is especially fine to walk in Muir Woods: the mosses are exceptionally beautiful and the dripping ferns give you the feeling of being in a proper rain forest. After a winter storm, the creeks run wild and the pungent smell of the redwoods seems to go right through your pores.

Since it is always a little cooler and damper in a redwood forest than anywhere else, dress warmly and keep your feet dry. By all means, take along whatever field guides you can—birds, wildflowers, ferns, trees—for Muir Woods is an extravagant outdoor museum. You will find a small hand lens particularly useful for examining mosses, lichens, ferns, and flowers.

The easiest walk down to Muir Woods begins near Mountain Home, following a paved access road down to Alice Eastwood Camp, then a foot path down Fern Creek Canyon to the national monument. The return back to Mountain Home is made via the *Ocean View Trail*, which manages to get back up the hill without ever being very taxing. Or if you wish, you can arrange a shuttle, leaving one car at the Muir Woods parking lot and driving a second car up to Mountain Home and the trailhead. Two other routes down to Muir Woods are described in the following chapter; these can also be used for possible return trips back up to the Panoramic Highway, though both are longer and more strenuous than the Ocean View Trail. The round trip described here is just over six miles long, so allow at least five hours to account for a lunch break, exploring the redwood giants of Muir Woods, and the extra time needed for the 700-foot climb back up the mountain.

From San Francisco, drive north on U.S. 101 across the Golden Gate Bridge to Marin County. Continue through the

Waldo Tunnel and down the grade on the other side. Just over two and one-half miles past the tunnel, take the exit reading "Mill Valley, Stinson Beach." (If driving south on U.S. 101, your exit is the first one after you cross Richardson Bay.) Head west on state highway 1—the Shoreline Highway—to a traffic signal about a half mile from the freeway. Turn left at the signal, following the Shoreline Highway for about three miles to its signed junction with the Panoramic Highway. Turn right at the junction and drive on Panoramic Highway for about three-fourths of a mile to the Muir Woods junction. *Do not turn left here unless you want to go to the main visitor area and park headquarters*. To get to the Mountain Home trailhead, continue on the Panoramic Highway for just under two miles to the California Alpine Club lodge, on your right. Watch for a locked bar gate on your left about 200 yards past the lodge; a sign reads "Alice Eastwood Camp—Organized Groups Only." This is the trailhead. Park in the clearing next to the gate or at the Mountain Home parking lot 200 feet up the highway. Bus service is available to Mountain Home, Bootjack Camp, and Pan Toll. Take the 62 (Bolinas) bus from the East Bay Terminal, at Fremont and Mission in San Francisco. For other stops in the city, and for exact schedules, call 332-6600.

Ignore the trail that heads off to Windy Gap from just this side of the gate. Skirt the gate and descend the paved *Old Railroad Grade* to Alice Eastwood Camp, which was named for the hearty botanist whose extensive fieldwork in Marin County around the turn of the century made her one of the foremost authorities on the county's flora. Here, your route is a wide auto track, which lacks the charm of the narrow woodland trail you will follow most of the way down to Muir Woods. But the views are spectacular from this stretch, and there is much along the route to interest the amateur naturalist.

As you drop into the dense forest, notice the masses of redwood sorrel (*Oxalis oregana*) along the stream banks and under the trees. Resembling an out-sized shamrock, the handsome leaves are refreshing to nibble, for they taste similar to watercress. Redwood sorrel begins to bloom in February and reaches its climax in the warmer days of March and April, when dozens of pink and lavender flowers appear.

The first little wildflower to bloom in the redwood forest (sometimes as early as January) is the California toothwort or milk maid (*Dentaria californica*), whose delicate pink flowers light up the forest floor. At one time the roots of this plant were eaten as a pungent relish. Unlike the flower of the redwood sorrel, which folds up when touched by the sun, the milk maids bloom wherever there is filtered light.

After a third of a mile, you will come to a sharp bend in the road, where it crosses Fern Canyon Creek, and a junction with the *Troop 80 Trail*, which heads west, winding along Panoramic Highway to Bootjack Camp. Troop 80 did such a fine job on bridges and steps that you wish other "troops" would tackle other trails. Although the rain-fed streams are among the great attractions of Muir Woods, heavy storms also cause the greatest damage to woodland trails. Mud slides, rock slides, and an occasional downed tree are evidence of how saturated and unstable these steep slopes can be in winter. A really well-made trail, such as the Troop 80 Trail, helps make Tamalpais the joy it is to wander through.

Alice Eastwood Camp is set aside for organized groups

for overnight camping. The upper part of the camp (which is off the trail) is surrounded by madrones and offers a fine view of Mount Tamalpais. The lower camp, where the *Old Railroad Grade* makes a big swing to the right, has a protected, sunny view of the sea. Here and there are parts of concrete foundations of the old Muir Woods Inn, which was situated at the end of the old railroad line. This hotel marked the beginning of a one-time tourist's walk down into Muir Woods.

Several trails meet at Alice Eastwood Camp. You can take the *Sierra Trail* back up to Panoramic Highway or follow either the *Old Wagon Road* or *Dad Plevins* cut down to Muir Woods. But neither matches the beauty of the *Fern Creek Canyon Trail*, which leads off to your left from the picnic area at lower Alice Eastwood Camp. This used to be the main route for visitors to Muir Woods, but now the hiker can enjoy this beautiful walk undisturbed even on crowded Sundays. Once you trade the hard road surface of the Old Railroad Grade for the springy feeling of the redwood duff, your feet know they are finally in the forest.

Fern Creek Canyon Trail makes an easy descent into the ravine. As you go farther downstream the trees get larger and larger, until the real redwood giants stand on the floor of the forest by Redwood Creek. But even up here at 500 feet, the fire-blackened elders measure ten feet in diameter. The older trees twist more at the base, the bark curving around the burls in eddies and swirls. The trunks are so tall they give the illusion of growing straight.

Along the trail you can see where the large fire-charred redwoods appear to be almost hollowed out, but from the trunk and the root system young trees sprout and form a family that grows in a close circle, reaching toward the

light. It is difficult not be anthropormorphic about redwoods, but when you see the parent tree so old and scarred
giving life to the next generation—and a generation is
measured as a thousand years—then reverence becomes
appropriate.

The sound of Fern Canyon Creek rushing along drowns
out the sound of the wind in the tops of the trees. Narrow
sunlight shafts pierce the forest, highlighting the creek as it
appears and dissappears into its shallow gorge. The clear
water falls from lips of rocks into foaming whirlpools;
cascades break over boulders, splitting off only to join
together again. It is hypnotic to sit on one of the big
comfortable streamside rocks in the sun and watch the
wearing force of the water. The stream is crossed by foot
bridges of dark redwood edged with moss. The bottom of
the ravine is strewn with fallen trees that make natural
bridges across the creek.

Resistant as the redwoods are to fire, insects, and decay,
the water that is so essential to their life can destroy them
when spring floods undermine their relatively shallow root
systems. It is hard to guess just how long a fallen redwood
tree has been down. After the first year a thick mat of moss
covers the whole log. Here and there new redwood sprouts
grow straight up to find light, while ferns and the starched,
shiny leaves of huckleberry fill the spaces.

The floor of the canyon, where the trail just rambles back
and forth across the creek, is the best place to have lunch.
Find a spot in the sun and settle down to watch the water
careen over the rocks, tossing the ferns with its spray. There
are nice surprises close at hand. Just near a fallen log look
for the Pacific trillium (*Trillum ovatum*), whose fragrance is
heavy and languorous, inappropriate to the nunlike wimple

of the white trefoil flower set against its three dark shiny leaves. Overhead, the catkins of California hazel move slightly in currents of air around the stream. Clinging to every forked stem is a small white spider in the very center of its orb web. You will notice a variety of mosses, some with small hairy cups, others growing in rosettes, still others in thick overlapping mats with the young fiddleheads of ferns, which uncoil like cobras from pockets of earth. There are not many mushrooms in the redwood forest, perhaps because the wood is so resistant to decay. But of the ones that do grow here, the most outstanding is the red hygrophorus (*Hygrophorus puniceus*), with its thick yellow-orange stem, creamy gills, and bright scarlet cap. Another red-capped mushroom, slimy to touch and extremely peppery to taste, is the *Russuala emetica. Both of these fungi are considered poisonous*, but the crimson caps along the trails are unexpected bright spots.

Like a small boy skipping back and forth across the stream, the trail ambles on until it reaches the sign, "Muir Woods National Monument." Until now you have been in Mount Tamalpais State Park. Just a little farther on, to the left, is a giant Douglas fir (*Pseudotsuga taxifolia*), so large that the first limbs seem nearly out of sight. Nearby is a large boulder that was brought down from the upper slopes of Mt. Tam, loaded on the train, carried down the mountain in a wagon, and finally rolled into place by dozens of people. It bears a bronze plaque dedicating this Douglas fir to William Kent, the father of Muir Woods and a man so modest that he would not allow President Theodore Roosevelt to name the monument for him, but suggested instead the name of John Muir, a man he had never met.

Continue along the trail to the park headquarters, where

you can get a piece of pie and a cup of coffee at the cafeteria, purchase some field guides for the area, or merely look at the educational displays. When you are ready to head back, retrace your steps along Redwood Creek to the Pinchot Memorial Grove on your right. Here the Ocean View Trail heads up to Mountain Home; a sign reads, "Panoramic Highway 2 miles." This route offers no ocean view until you reach the big rock at the top, but it does pass through a tranquil, little-traveled canyon of smaller redwoods. At first, the trail climbs steeply, but soon, though it never ceases climbing, it assumes a more reasonable grade. At first you are walking through redwoods, but as you gain elevation these give way to Douglas fir, tanoak, oaks, and madrone. Watch for the comparatively uncommon California nutmeg (*Torreya californica*) along this trail. You can recognize it by its large, bright green, sharply pointed needles, and in the right season, by its plumlike seeds. Although it superficially resembles a conifer, it has no cones. The Ocean View Trail is fast and pleasant, if not spectacular.

After you pass the big rock near the top of the climb, you will come out across the road from the California Alpine Club. From there it is just a short walk up the road to your car. And from there you can walk downstairs from Bootjack Camp to Muir Woods along the most vivacious stream on the south side of Mount Tamalpais.

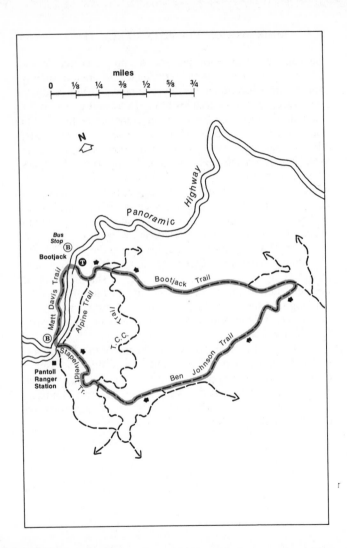

7. BOOTJACK TO MUIR WOODS

The *Bootjack Trail*, which begins directly across the high-way from the parking lot at Bootjack Camp, is a steep descent into the canyon of Redwood Creek through a forest of redwood, Douglas fir, madrone, tanoak, California laurel, and big-leaf maple. It is a route crowded with ferns and boasting some of the most beautiful wildflower displays of all the back trails into Muir Woods. It is a good hike on a hot day because you are walking in the shade most of the way. It is good on a windy or rainy day because the tall, dense forest offers excellent protection from all but the fiercest storms. But it is best on a mild day in spring, when the sun filters to the forest floor in long glimmering shafts and the wildflowers shine back in response.

In the 1930s the Civilian Conservation Corps laid great serpentine rock steps along the first half mile of the trail. Below that, as the trail gets even steeper, the roots of big redwoods themselves become the steps of a giant staircase. Though the Bootjack Trail is great to go down, it is anguish for many hikers on their way up. Just when they are really bushed, the trail gets even steeper, the steps higher and farther apart.

Fortunately, you do not have to return via the Bootjack Trail. In fact, you have three other good choices, including the Fern Creek Canyon Trail and the Ocean View Trail (see Section 6). But the most convenient way to avoid going back up the Bootjack Trail is to take the *Ben Johnson Trail* up to Pan Toll. From there, it is an easy half-mile walk back to your car in the parking lot at Bootjack Camp. The entire trip is about four and one-quarter miles. The Ben Johnson Trail is longer than the Bootjack, but much more gradual.

There are no stretches along this trail as steep as the Bootjack Steps and only a few places where the ascent is at all difficult. The trail winds gradually up the south slope of a stream canyon and almost invariably takes the route of least resistance.

From San Francisco, drive north on U.S. 101 to the Stinson Beach/Mill Valley exit. Turn left at the first stop light, about a half mile from the freeway. Drive for almost three miles to the junction with the Panoramic Highway, which heads off to the right. Take this road up to Bootjack Camp. You will come first to the Muir Woods junction. The road on your left heads down to park headquarters, the road on your right down to Mill Valley. The Panoramic Highway here makes a slight jog to the left, winding up to Mountain Home in one and two-thirds miles. Bootjack Camp is two and one-third miles beyond Mountain Home; the parking lot is on your right. Walk directly across the highway to the sign reading "Bootjack Trail to Muir Woods." Bus service is available to Mountain Home, Bootjack Camp, and Pan Toll. Take the 62 (Bolinas) bus from the East Bay Terminal, at Fremont and Mission in San Francisco. For other stops in the city, and for exact schedules, call 332-6600.

The trail immediately begins to switchback down through a mixed forest of redwoods and California laurel, crossing a tiny creek twice via footbridges before coming to the junction with the *Alpine Trail* to Pan Toll. Keep left, winding down to another apparent trail junction. A sign points left to the Bootjack Trail, which now begins to switchback more steeply down into the canyon. The forest assumes a parklike atmosphere as you descend to another stream.

After crossing the footbridge over the creek you will

come shortly to the first of two junctions with the Troop 80 Trail, which heads east, paralleling the Panoramic Highway. It intersects the *Sierra Trail* in just over a mile, and the Old Railroad Grade (see Section 6) in just under two miles. Just beyond the Troop 80 Trail junction, you meet the first Douglas firs along this trail. From here down to Muir Woods, you will notice that the redwoods tend to grow more thickly near the streams, while the Douglas firs dominate the higher, drier slopes.

The trail leaves the deep woods for a short way, winding through an open sunny area, then descending some rock steps lined with miner's lettuce (*Montia perfoliata*). This edible member of the purslane family grows abundantly in open woodlands throughout the Bay Area, as well as in the Sierra and much of the rest of California. It has a tangy flavor that would go nicely with oil and vinegar. You can recognize it by the round leaves, which have small stems emerging from their very centers. In the spring each stem bears a tiny white flower.

Soon, if you take this hike in the winter or spring, you will hear the roar of Redwood Creek as it tumbles down the canyon. When you come to a log fence at a bend in the trail, you can see the stream through the woods. Just beyond the fence, you enter Van Wyck Meadow, the only real opening in the forest along this entire walk. The meadow is surrounded by Douglas firs and dotted with several large serpentine boulders. This would be an excellent place for lunch if it were not so close to the beginning of the trail. It is a fine place to stretch out in the sun, in any case. Birds are plentiful here, at the forest's edge, and you might want to tary long enough to check them out.

Just after entering the meadow, the *T.C.C. Trail* heads

off to the right. This trail winds through deep forest for one and three-fourths miles to the *Dipsea Trail*. It crosses the Ben Johnson Trail en route, marking the spot where, on your way up to Pan Toll Camp, you pick up the *Stapelveldt Trail*. At the far corner of the meadow the second fork of the Troop 80 Trail takes off, meeting the first fork a short way beyond. The Bootjack Trail heads straight through the meadow, then drops via rock steps past a dense grove of young redwoods to the edge of Redwood Creek. For most of the rest of the way to Muir Woods, the trail closely parallels Redwood Creek, a picturesque stream given to energetic cascades among serpentine boulders covered with ferns.

From here on the giant stairway begins in earnest, and at first it is an amusing novelty. After a mile or so of this steep descent, however, most people are happy when the trail finally levels out. Be careful on the way down, especially during winter and spring, when the steps can be slippery.

During the spring this descent is bright with wildflowers, though in dense woods they seldom provide the mass displays that are typical of open grasslands. But the number of species, if not of individual flowers, is impressive. Most common here, as all over Mt. Tam, are Pacific hound's tongue, foetid adder's tongue, star lily, redwood sorrel, and trillium. Other species found in this canyon include the redwood violet, fairy lantern, clintonia, and anemone, The western azalea (*Rhododendron occidentale*), a spectacular plant in late spring, grows as an understory shrub in Muir Woods and Bootjack Canyon, but is not abundant in either place. Its showy white flowers can be seen in May or June. Ferns of the area include western sword fern (*Polystichum munitum*), which grows in huge bouquets along the stream;

chain fern (*Woodwardia fimbriata*), which is also common along Redwood Creek; licorice fern (*Polypodium glycyr-rhiza*), which you can find growing on boulders along the way; and California maidenhair (*Adiantum jordani*), which will require some searching. Nor are these the only ferns along this trail. To distinguish all of them, take along a good field guide and a hand lens. In all, about twenty species of ferns have been identified on Mount Tamalpais.

After crossing a footbridge over a tributary to Redwood Creek, you begin to notice very large redwoods and Douglas firs. One old fir, located right beside the trail, is about six feet across at the base, and the first real branches don't occur until thirty feet or so up the trunk. Here the tree has formed a second trunk of sorts, while yet another branch winds upward in a contorted fashion. Just beyond the tree, a narrow path leads uphill on your left. Keep to your right and come shortly to a footbridge where a side stream has eroded away much of the cliff. Then cross Redwood Creek itself and drop into an open grove of small redwoods and Douglas firs.

Here the trail gets really steep, dropping in giant steps down to another bridge over Redwood Creek. The source of the lumber for this bridge must be a subject of speculation for virtually every hiker who crosses it, for clearly written on the downstream railing is the bold legend, "Surf Unsafe." The view from here, both up and down the stream, is magnificent. Above the water comes cascading down the canyon through dense woods, only to level out for awhile in an open stretch beyond the bridge. On the south bank is the first big-leaf maple (*Acer macrophyllum*) you meet along this walk. Its bright green leaves in spring, or bright gold ones in autumn, stand out boldly from the deep green of the surrounding conifers. The maple seems to shine with a light of its own. You will encounter more maples as you walk downstream.

Shortly after the bridge the trail levels out, along with Redwood Creek, which now meanders down a wide, sunny streambed. It then drops more steeply for one last stretch before finally leveling out as it approaches the boundary of Muir Woods. You will notice that the vegetation is somewhat different along this stretch. Ferns and mosses no longer dominate the streamside scene; willows and maples are increasingly common; and horsetails line the boggier stretches of the trail. In the forest itself, maples and California laurels assume fantastic shapes in their attempts to steal sunlight from the overbearing redwoods.

The first recorded mention of the coast redwoods was made by Father Juan Crespi in 1769. In his journal of the Portola expedition he describes "very high trees of a red color, not known to us. They have a very different leaf from cedars, and although the wood resembles cedar somewhat in color, it is very different, and has not the same odor; moreover, the wood of the trees that we have found is very brittle. In this region there is a great abundance of these trees and because none of the expedition recognizes them, they are named redwood from their color."

The first botanical specimens were brought back to England in 1795 by Archibald Menzies, who sailed on the Vancouver expedition as both surgeon and botanist. But the specimens gathered dust in England until 1823, when an English botanist, thinking them related to the bald cypress, assigned them to the genus *Taxodium* and named this new species *sempervirens*, meaning "ever living," (sometimes, mistakenly, "ever green"). His mistake was corrected by an Austrian botanist in 1847, who recognized them as members of a new genus, which he named *Sequoia* after the great Cherokee educator *Sequo-yah*. Until quite recently the genus *Sequoia* was thought to include two species: *Sequoia*

sempervirens, the coast redwood, and *Sequoia gigantea*, the Big Tree of the Sierra. Now, the latter belongs to a separate genus and is known as *Sequoiadendron giganteum*.

Early claims for the age of the coast redwood ranged up to 5,000 years, but more recent estimates place the age of the oldest known redwood at 2,200 years. In Muir Woods, estimates range up to 1,500 years; some of the trees may be older. Size is not a reliable sign of age, which also depends on other factors, such as soil conditions and exposure. Two redwoods of the same size and from the same forest may be centuries apart in age.

Just before you enter Muir Woods National Monument, you pass a trail on your left leading up to Alice Eastwood Camp. Keep right, passing the park boundary sign and the Andrew J. Cross tree on your left. Shortly you will come to a fork in the trail. The left fork continues along Redwood Creek, through the main section of Muir Woods, to the park headquarters. The right fork crosses Redwood Creek on a footbridge and continues as the *Ben Johnson Trail*. Which fork you take depends on what you want to do.

If you decide to walk to park headquarters, continue on the Bootjack Trail, which shortly turns into a less-than-charming paved path. If you have not encountered many people up till now, you surely will on this one-mile walk along Redwood Creek. When William Kent donated this grove to the people of the United States in 1908, he scarcely could have imagined that some 800,000 of them would come each year to walk this trail. The Park Service has had to fence off certain overtrod areas to protect the plants and animals, and has forbidden picnicking within the park boundaries. Although it is easy to understand why so many people visit this splendid grove, the weekend and holiday crowds do pose a problem for the hiker seeking a measure of solitude. This is why the back trails down to Muir Woods are so delightful. They allow you to experience the redwood forest on a one-to-one basis, without the distractions of buildings, pavement, fences, and too many of your own species. The Ben Johnson Trail, your route from this fork, has redwoods that nearly equal in size those along Redwood Creek.

If you need to orient yourself, a map posted at the bridge by the Park Service shows all the main trails. Cross the bridge and continue uphill past a trail that has been closed according to the sign, "to restore to nature." Shortly thereafter, you will pass the *Hillside Trail*, which comes in on your left. (This trail avoids the pavement and fences on its way down to the park headquarters. It is a good route back, should you decide to visit the headquarters on some future walk.) The uphill grade is easy so far and the trail is well laid out, as it is all the way up.

Climb moderately through redwoods, laurels, and tan-oaks, crossing a small stream and rounding a ridge, where clintonia blooms along the trail. The grade levels out somewhat, and through the trees on your right you get fleeting glimpses of distant ridges and the summit of Mount Tamalpais. This section of the trail is lined with wood ferns, lady ferns, and huckleberries. Cross a stream on a bridge between two redwoods, then two small gullies that carry seasonal trickles. Climb gradually for about a half mile to another stream and a pipe with water flowing from it. A sign reads: "Stream used for drinking water. Please keep it clean." Opposite the stream is a huge hollowed-out redwood that is as impressive as most of the specimens down in the more heavily traveled sections of the park. You will notice all along this trail that the redwoods seem to be larger than those that lined your route down Bootjack Canyon.

From here the trail gets steeper, and you can hear the stream in the canyon below. You come shortly to a side trail leading uphill on your left to the *Dipsea Trail*. Keep right, climbing steeply through fine old redwoods. The trail levels out again just above a small stream. Cross several dry side streams, then climb again before finally meeting the larger creek on the right, just before a series of steep switchbacks up the ridge on your left. Do not cut across the switchbacks, as many hikers have already done, for this will hasten the erosion of this steep slope. At the first turn you will come to a narrow side trail; keep left. The trail climbs steeply to the T.C.C. and Stapelveldt trails. First you come to the segment of the *T.C.C. Trail* that leads south to the Dipsea Trail; this leaves the *Ben Johnson Trail* at a sharp angle on your left. Stay right at this junction; just ahead, the T.C.C. Trail continues on your right, crossing a bridge and heading north to meet the Bootjack Trail at Van Wyck Meadow. This is a possible loop back to your car. To continue up to Pan Toll, turn left just before the bridge on the *Stapelveldt Trail*. The junction is signed.

The Stapelveldt Trail climbs steeply through a thicket of tall, skinny California laurels, crossing three footbridges before making a big steep bend to the right over the ridge crest. Here, the forest is noticeably drier and is dominated by big sprawling Douglas firs. For the first time live oaks also appear in the forest mix. As you walk in oak litter, the first campsite at Pan Toll, the only public campground on Mt. Tam, appears on your left above the trail. Shortly you will come to a paved campground path running along a log fence. Cross this and head into the shrubby woods. From here it is a short descent to the parking lot at Pan Toll. To get back to Bootjack Camp, either pick up the *Alpine Trail* right where you come to the parking lot or walk across Panoramic Highway to take the *Matt Davis Trail*, which heads right just above the road. The Alpine Trail is a little longer and involves a brief uphill stretch after it meets the Bootjack Trail, just below the parking lot. Either trail is an easy walk back to your car.

8. MOUNTAIN HOME TO EAST PEAK

Beginning at Mountain Home, this moderately strenuous loop is perhaps the best way to climb to the top of Mount Tamalpais, for unlike most of the other possible routes, it is never ridiculously steep. Along the way you are treated to fabulous views of San Francisco, Marin County, the ocean, and the bay, and you visit a quaint old inn set all by itself on a wooded promontory on the south slope of the mountain. On your way back, you descend via a lush streamside woodland where you are sure to find solitude amidst the ferns and cascades. The average family will not find any part of this walk too difficult, and on each leg of the hike you have a definite goal to look forward to. Allow three to four hours, depending on how long you take for lunch, stops at waterfalls, and rests at the more spectacular views.

Briefly, here is your route; from Mountain Home, take the *Throckmorton Trail* north up the mountain to the *Old Railroad Grade*, where you turn left and walk to West Point. Continuing on the *Old Railroad Grade*, you climb from West Point to the highway leading to East Peak, the summit of Mount Tamalpais. You can either walk up the road and climb the peak for one of the most spectacular views in the Bay Area, or you can immediately follow the *Fern Creek Trail* down to rejoin the Old Railroad Grade below West Point and retrace your steps back to Mountain Home. This three and one-half mile semiloop trip is easy uphill, interesting downhill, and seldom repetitive.

From San Francisco, drive north on U.S. 101 to the

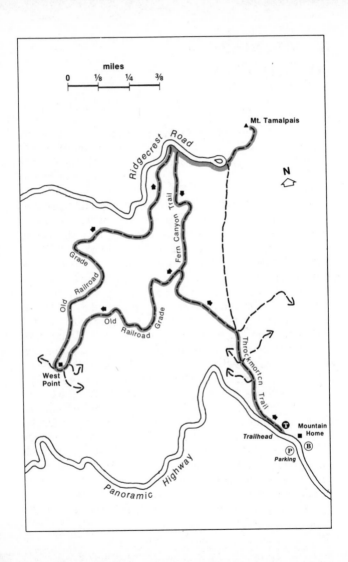

Stinson Beach/Mill Valley exit. Turn left at the first stop-light about half a mile from the freeway. Drive for almost three miles to the junction with the Panoramic Highway, which heads off to the right. Take this road up to Mountain Home, a distance of about two and one-half miles. Park in the lots on the left side of the highway. Bus service is available to Mountain Home, Bootjack Camp, and Pan Toll. Take the 62 (Bolinas) bus from the East Bay Terminal, at Fremont and Mission in San Francisco. For other stops in the city, and for exact schedules, call 332-6600.

The *Throckmorton Trail* leaves the Panoramic Highway just above Mountain Home, cutting a reddish swath up the side of Mount Tam through manzanita, coyote bush, and Scotch and French broom. Imported from Europe, Scotch broom (*Cystius scoparius*) has become an invasive pest in many parts of northern California, including the slopes of Tamalpais, but in the early spring its brilliant yellow flowers almost make up for its otherwise unfortunate habits. Manzanita is a native, whose attractiveness lies more in its shiny purple bark and often picturesque shapes than in its rather modest flowers. In January the manzanita bushes are full of tiny waxy pink bells, which open into small rosy urns on the first warm days of spring and provide a great feast for bees.

Here on the Throckmorton Trail, the manzanita is knee high; later on this hike, different species will tower over your head. There are so many kinds of manzanita that learning all the different varieties could be a pastime in itself. Mount Tamalpais has six species, ranging from carpetlike groundcovers to small trees. Indian children apparently considered the red berries that appear in late August a sweet treat, though most people would probably find them rather too woody and bitter. It is also possible to brew a sour drink from the berries, which is then sweetened with sugar, much like lemonade.

About a third of a mile from Mountain Home you pass signs on the left pointing out the *Nora Trail* and *Matt Davis Trail*. For hikers who prefer not to climb East Peak, a possible loop from here is to take the Matt Davis Trail to Bootjack Camp and then return to Mountain Home on the Troop 80 Trail. The Nora Trail branches from the Matt Davis Trail and climbs steeply up to West Point, which you will reach via Old Railroad Grade.

After passing the junction with the *Hoo Koo E Koo Trail*, you come shortly to the fire road that now runs along the Old Railroad Grade. Turn left and head for West Point, an old-fashioned hikers' club that invites visitors to use its veranda for lunch and rest. Along this stretch of trail, late winter brings a showy display of violet ceanothus. The rocks are warm and sheltered on this sea side of the mountain, so much so that they have created little micro-climates warm enough to force the ceanothus to bloom at least six weeks before it would in shadier, cooler locations. Blue blossom (*Ceanothus thyrsiflorus*), which may be a prostrate mat, shrub, or small tree depending on growing conditions, lives up to its name each spring. Called the California lilac, its masses of deep blue flowers are much beloved by people and bees. It also harbors the wood tick, so take care if you wish a closer look. Mt. Tam has several varieties of ceanothus, ranging in color from pinkish-white to a deep blue-violet. You will see several species in the chaparral on this trip.

During the winter, rains can turn quiet mountain springs into cascades and waterfalls that are wonderful to look at. There are several on the way to West Point, and giant chain ferns grow thick along these rushing little streams. If you examine the back side of a chain fern frond, you will see that the sori (spore sacks) are linked together in a definite chain pattern.

Shortly after leaving the Throckmorton Trail, the Old Railroad Grade crosses the west fork of Fern Creek, where the predominant shrub vegetation suddenly gives way to a woodland of madrones and redwood, with some Douglas firs and California laurels mixed in. One beautiful madrone has a trunk that forms a continuous spiral—an art nouveau tree. The madrone (*Arbutus menziesii*), like the manzanita, is a member of the heath family, and both have smooth, skinlike bark, which varies from eggplant color in the manzanita to orange in the madrone. Both also have waxy bell-like flowers. Madrone berries are bright red and much loved by birds. Its leaves, unlike the manzanita's, are broad and smooth, somewhat resembling those of a magnolia. You will encounter the madrone throughout the area covered by this book, sometimes mixed with redwoods or Douglas firs, sometimes with other broadleaf evergreen trees, such as the California laurel and tanoak. The Indians, who relished the madrone's berries, are said to have regarded it as a sacred tree.

After Fern Creek, the fire road winds gently around the mountain for about three-quarters of a mile in chaparral and occasional woods to West Point, which has been a resting spot for hikers since 1912. You can eat lunch on the sheltered porch and buy some lemonade, tea, or coffee from one of the club members. It is a good place to rest, looking out through the pines to the ocean. In the old days, the Muir Woods and Tamalpais Railroad stopped here on its way to the top of the peak.

If you wish to turn back at West Point, a possible loop is to take the Nora Trail to the Matt Davis Trail, which you follow east back to the Throckmorton Trail and Mountain Home. To take the Nora Trail, walk straight across the Old Railroad Grade from the veranda of the West Point Inn. The trailhead is signed. To the right of the Nora Trail, the *Old Stage Road* takes off for Bootjack Camp; and to the right of that, the *Rock Springs Trail* heads off in the chaparral, bound for the Mountain Theater.

Follow the Old Railroad Grade around the inn and begin climbing through chaparral. In about half a mile the trail rounds a ridge and drops into the wooded canyon of Fern Creek, climbing out the other side back into chaparral and on up to the highway about a quarter mile below the parking lot. If you wish to take the easy trail to the top of East Peak, head up the highway to the parking lot, where the route is well marked. On a clear day you can see as far south as Monterey Bay and east to Mount Diablo and beyond. To the west, the green pastoral landscape of west Marin rolls gently to the sea. Right below you to the north you can see the sparkling reservoirs of the Marin Municipal Water District nestling in woods and grassy hills.

In choosing your route down the mountain, avoid both the Throckmorton and the Telephone trails. The first is nothing more than a steep, straight, red slash of loose rocks; you cannot enjoy the view if you have to watch your feet. The second is loose dirt marked by telephone poles, not exactly the right motif for a mountain trail. But the *Fern Creek Trail* is a joy, even if it is hard to find. It is not now marked, but you will find it heading down the mountain about a hundred feet up the highway from the Old Railroad Grade. Look for a footpath over a cut in the road.

Pick up the trail as it starts off through the knee-high manzanita. Directly on your left, you can see a line of telephone poles going down through a canyon. Farther on your left, you can see the *Throckmorton Trail*, which goes over two hills before sliding down. Fern Creek Trail keeps to the left side of a knoll on the mountain. You will soon see some water pipes low down on the left side of the trail. The manzanita gets waist high and then higher as you go down the mountain. At one place you reach a water tank with good water at the spigot all year long. Here you should follow the trail to your left through a dense undergrowth of manzanita, bay trees, and madrones. You can see where countless hikers have made easy hand grips on the silky madrone trunks, which are irresistible to the touch.

As the sound of Fern Creek gets louder and louder, the moss gets as thick as fur, and the rocks become even more picturesque than before. The roots of bay trees twist all over the rocks, leaving small doorways dripping with moss and miniature gardens of ferns with footpaths of small stones, and an occasional crimson or lavender mushroom.

At the old stone bridge the creek goes wild, having tossed huge boulders around for several hundred years. The redwood trees appear by the fire road and the half mad, enchanted part of the trail abruptly cuts off into a more human world. Turn to the left on the fire road and follow it to the point where it joins the end of the Throckmorton Trail, leading back to Mountain Home.

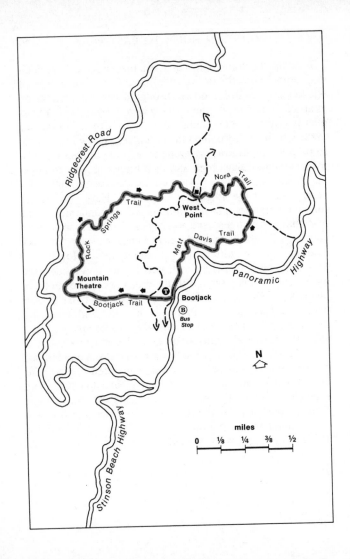

9. BOOTJACK CAMP
TO WEST POINT

West Point, a welcome halfway house on the preceding hike, is your destination on this loop. The hospitality of the old club's veranda and lemonade will be a welcome touch of civilization on this otherwise wild hike through the woods and chaparral of Mount Tamalpais. The view from the inn is incredible, stretching from the distant Berkeley hills on the east to the vast Pacific on the west, and in between, the broad sweep of San Francisco Bay and the cities clustered around it.

You may choose from among several routes for this hike, none of them particularly taxing. The most difficult one, described in detail below, is still an easy morning or afternoon jaunt, involving only a short, though admittedly steep uphill stretch of trail between Bootjack Camp and Mountain Theater. Anyone in reasonably good shape should be able to manage this hike easily, but for those who prefer even less strenuous routes, fine alternatives exist.

Early spring is the best time to make this hike because the wildflowers are more plentiful and the streams more active than earlier or later in the year. Avoid this walk on a hot day because much of it covers exposed brushy slopes. Allow two to four hours depending on the route you choose and other intangibles, such as your capacity for lemonade.

Though we suggest beginning this hike at Bootjack Camp on Panoramic Highway, you can just as easily begin from Mountain Theater on Ridgecrest Road. To get to Bootjack Camp, take the Stinson Beach exit off U.S. 101 north of San Francisco. Drive a half mile to a stoplight and turn left. You are on state highway 1, the Shoreline Highway. Follow

the highway for about two and a half miles to the junction
with the Panoramic Highway. Turn right at this fork. In
about two miles, pass Mountain Home on your right.
Continue up the mountain for about another two and a half
miles to the parking lot at Bootjack Camp, located just off
the right side of the highway. Bus service is available to
Mountain Home, Bootjack Camp, and Pan Toll. Take the
62 (Bolinas) bus from the East Bay Terminal, at Fremont
and Mission in San Francisco. For other stops in the city,
and for exact schedules, call 332-6600.

From the parking lot, walk up through the picnic area to a
clearing at the far end. Here, you will see two trails.
Straight ahead, next to a broad track running steeply uphill,
is a sign reading "Bootjack Trail to Mountain Theater."
This is your trail if you want to walk the steep portion of the
hike at the start. After climbing 450 feet in just over a half
mile, you have nothing but gentle ups and a lot of downs to
contend with. (If you wish to postpone the uphill portion for
a time, take the Matt Davis Trail, which heads into the
woods on your right. It winds around the mountain pretty
much on the level, meeting the *Nora Trail* at Laguna Creek,
about a mile away. Turning on the Nora Trail, you climb
very steeply to West Point.)

Walk uphill on the Bootjack Trail to just below the ranger
residence. Keep left through the trees, cross a dirt road
leading up to the house, and climb gently through cool
woods to meet the same road farther uphill. Turn left on the
road. When you intersect another road in a clearing, turn
right. You will see two signs. The more conspicuous one
reads "*R and H Trail*." A smaller one on the right of the
road a few yards before the "R and H" sign points left to
the Bootjack Trail, which leaves the road here to climb a

steep set of rock stairs. This is your route. The R and H Trail is really the Old Stage Road to West Point (the "R and H" stand for the obvious—riding and hiking).

For an easier route to and from West Point than the one described here, start at Mountain Theater, walk down the Bootjack Trail to this junction, and take the Old Stage Road to West Point. You can return to Mountain Theater via the easy Rock Springs Trail. By taking this route, you will cut perhaps a mile or more off the suggested hike, but you will miss the ferns, redwoods, and lovely streams that mark the Nora Trail, and you will have traded a pleasant footpath for a wide red swath.

Continuing up the Bootjack Trail, climb steeply through a clearing, where the view is panoramic, and then back into woods of oak, Douglas fir, tanoak, and madrone, a combination you will meet several times during this hike. From here, the trail is obvious and steep, but thankfully not too long. Soon you will come to Mountain Theater, the second possible trailhead for this hike.

Walk along the top row of seats, ignoring the picturesque amphitheater and splendid view long enough to notice a signpost on your left confirming that you are on the "Rock Springs Trail to West Point."

After passing the last seat, you meet the trail proper, which moves in and out of woods and chaparral as it winds its way around the south side of the mountain. Here the woods are predominantly tanoak and young Douglas firs; the chaparral is dominated by chamise, toyon, and ceanothus. Later, both woods and chaparral will assume a somewhat different aspect. Look for Pacific houndstongue, star lilies, and Douglas iris along the way. In the moister stretches, you will discover lady ferns, chain ferns, and sword ferns. Bracken is common all along the trail. Trillium grow in the damp, stream-cut ravines.

This trail is remarkable for its variety of terrain, vegetation, and views. Intimate woodland corridors suddenly give way to fifty-mile prospects over the chaparral. Your attention alternates between the delicate subtleties of a shaded flower and the overwhelming impact of a world at your feet. You cross gray-green serpentine barrens, only to idle minutes later by a rushing stream amid dense stands of laurel and oak.

The trail runs nearly level all the way to West Point, with only minor ups and downs as it rounds gentle ridges and descends into stream canyons. The trail crosses four large streams and several minor trickles in its one and a half miles to the inn, but do not expect to see them flowing during the summer. At best, you will find a trickle where cascades once ran.

About halfway to West Point the composition of the chaparral changes abruptly from toyon, chamise, and ceanothus to manzanita, sometimes growing as low mats down the mountainside, sometimes as shrubs five or six feet tall. The various species of manzanita can be difficult for the amateur to identify with any confidence, though there are a few exceptions. But with some patience and a good set of botanical keys, you might be able to pick out two or three types along this trail.

West Point Inn comes into view long before you finally arrive. You will see it sitting amid a stand of pines on a modest promontory east and somewhat below you. It is an attractive goal, which seems farther away than it really is. The trail contours the ridges and canyons of the mountainside, but is always so easy that the distance passes

before you know it. The trail meets the Old Railroad Grade at the southwest corner of the inn.

After resting a spell—drinking lemonade, eating lunch, using the restrooms, whatever—you have several possible continuations to choose from. If you wish to continue on to East Peak, follow the fire road uphill around the west side of the inn, as described in the preceding hike. Or you can go to Mountain Home either by following the Old Railroad Grade east to the Throckmorton Trail, or by descending the Nora Trail to the Matt Davis Trail, which you also can take east to the Throckmorton Trail above Mountain Home. To complete the loop to Bootjack (or Mountain Theater), you can either take the Old Stage Road, a broad fire road that parallels the Rock Springs Trail at a lower elevation, or the Nora Trail, turning right at its junction with the Matt Davis Trail.

The Nora Trail is short but beautiful, crossing four or five streams on its steep winding descent to the Matt Davis Trail. The canyon of Laguna Creek is among the more picturesque on this side of the mountain. The stream fairly leaps down the canyon, which is thick with ferns and redwoods and some of the most impressive tanoaks to be found in the area. Fighting for light with the redwoods has impelled the tanoaks to favor long straight trunks—not their usual habit—much like those of aspens. The first branches on these trees were perhaps forty feet above the stream.

The junction with the Matt Davis Trail is a little tricky. After crossing the footbridge over Laguna Creek, the trail closely follows the east bank. Shortly you will come to a sign *facing the opposite direction* tacked to a tree on your right. Turn around and look at this sign: it marks the junction with the Matt Davis Trail and instructs you to cross the stream if you wish to go to Bootjack Camp. If you somehow miss the sign, you will know you have passed it when the trail begins to climb above the stream and a large serpentine boulder appears on your right. Turn around at this point and you cannot miss the sign.

From here to Bootjack Camp, the Matt Davis Trail runs mostly on the level, descending into wooded canyons and climbing around the ridges that separate them. This trail is perhaps more open than the Rock Springs Trail above, but it crosses the same number of streams on its way back to Bootjack. The chaparral seems thicker here, and though manzanita is common, you do not encounter the extensive low stretches of it that you do on the higher route.

As you wind in and out of the canyons and over the ridges, you will occasionally hear autos far below, winding their way up to Bootjack. Now and then you will get a glimpse of Panoramic Highway, but more often you are left merely with the panorama of mountainside and the sea. The trail is narrow, intimate, and well-graded, and in this respect it is preferable to the Old Stage Road. From West Point back to Bootjack along the Nora-Matt Davis route is about one and three-fourths miles.

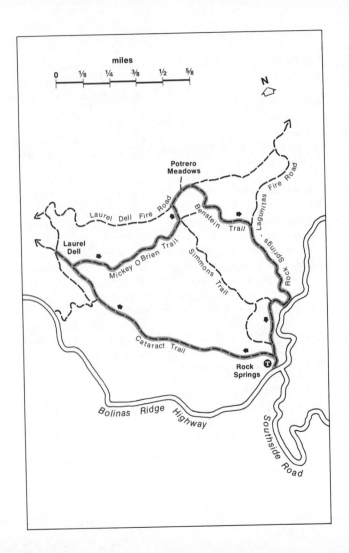

10. LAUREL DELL

The walk from Rock Springs to Laurel Dell is a delightful stroll along Cataract Creek. The trail winds gently downhill in and out of deep forests and sunny grasslands. Wildflowers are abundant in the streamside meadows, especially from March through May, when species follows species in a continuous cycle of bloom. You may want a picnic lunch to eat at Laurel Dell or Mountain Theater, comfortable walking shoes to take you up the short rocky climb on the *Benstein Trail*, a lens for looking at the smaller wildflowers, and any field guides you choose to carry. Since this is a good walk for birds. you might also bring your binoculars.

From San Francisco, drive north on U.S. 101 to the Mill Valley/Stinson Beach exit. Leave the freeway and drive west for a half mile to an intersection with a traffic light. Turn left, and in about three miles, turn right on Panoramic Highway, which heads up the mountain. In five miles, you will come to an intersection with the Southside Road at Pan Toll. Follow the sign that reads, "Mount Tamalpais, 4 miles." In one and a half miles you will come to Rock Springs. Park in the dirt lot directly across the highway. You can reverse this walk by parking at Mountain Theater, just up the road to your right, and walking up the highway about 200 feet to the red gate on your left, which marks Lagunitas Road.

From the Rock Springs parking lot, go through the wooden turnstile, just beyond which you will come to three trails. The one on your right goes to Mountain Theater. The middle one, the *Simon Trail*, heads directly down to Barth's Retreat. It is an interesting alternate route to the one described here, but because it lacks a creek, wildflowers are never so abundant. You want the trail on your left, which is signed "Laurel Dell via Cataract Gulch." You will know for sure that you are on the right path when you pass a wooden water tank on your left and cross a foot-span creek.

The walk is about three miles in all, so you can easily make it in two to three hours, including time on your stomach looking at wildflowers, making side trips up animal trails to see the Pacific, or sunning yourself on a lichen-covered boulder. There is drinking water along the way, with taps at Laurel Dell, Potrero Meadows, Barth's Retreat, and Mountain Theater.

Most of this hike and the next one are on the watershed lands of the Marin Municipal Water District, which generously allows hikers to wander over their extensive holdings (some 50,000 acres), but its first concern, of course, is protecting the natural cover of the watershed. Hikers are therefore forbidden, as they are in adjacent state and federal lands, to remove or disturb plants and animals, to pollute streams, or to build fires except in designated grills. Since these lands provide water for most of Marin County's residents, you cannot be too careful to follow the simple rules. Dogs are not allowed on the trails.

Rock Springs is a wide meadow crossed by Zeiche Creek and Cataract Creek. On bright Sundays it is full of people picnicking, throwing frisbees, playing guitars, or just lying on the grass watching hawks ride the thermals. The open picnic area is within a few feet of the parking lot, so the area is very popular with families. But head down the *Cataract Trail*, and you soon leave most of the people behind.

The trail along Cataract Creek down to Laurel Dell is generally an open footpath down a canyon wooded with oaks, tanoaks, Douglas firs, madrones, and laurels. In

places it skirts big boulders right at the water's edge. The creek alternately rushes down the canyon and winds lazily through wet grasslands, which are lush with wildflowers.

During the spring you may be accompanied by clouds of butterflies, especially if the previous fall has brought one of the periodic—and unexplained—population explosions of the California tortoiseshell (*Nymphalis californica*), which occasionally winter on Mount Tamalpais in enormous numbers. In some years they may be comparatively scarce. These rather small brown and orange butterflies, newly released from their chrysalides, stretch their wings and fan them back and forth in the sun, or flutter in erratic crowds over the brush. Ceanothus and coffee berry (*Rhamnus californica*), both members of the buckthorn family, are the tortoiseshell's main food. Other butterflies you may see include the tiny Acmon blue (*Plebejus acmon*) or the spring azure (*Celastrina argiolus*)—both measuring about an inch from wing tip to wing tip, though the Acmon blue may even be smaller.

With any luck you should be able to find magenta shooting stars along Cataract Creek, for in places these beautiful members of the primrose family grow thickly along the stream. They vary in color from pale pink to deepest purple, usually rising on five-to-ten-inch stems, with three shooting stars showing down. Their botanical name (*Dodecatheon hendersonii*) reflects an old tradition that these elegant flowers were favored by the gods (*Dodeca*—"twelve" and *theon*—"gods"; in other words, the twelve gods of Olympus). In the early days, when most people were not so careful about their nomenclature, shooting stars were known variously as "mad violets," "prairie pointers," "mosquito bills," and "rooster heads," the last apparently the designation of prosaic little boys who would hook the blossoms together and pull to see which flower head would come off first. It is hard to imagine so many shooting stars in California that little boys would be able to find enough "rooster heads" to play games with.

The trail from Rock Springs drops 500 feet in just over a mile to the large grassland known as Laurel Dell. You can stretch out on the grass right next to the creek, with shooting stars your jaunty companions. This sunny place is ideal for eating your lunch, whether next to the stream or at the picnic tables nearby, where tap water and latrines are available. There is a grill for cooking, if you like. The next best place for lunch may be Mountain Theater itself. Perhaps you would rather walk unburdened, saving a leisurely lunch for your return to the theater, where you can spread a cloth out on the warm serpentine rocks and look out across the bay.

Picnics, of course, are everywhere associated with ants, and though these pose little problem at Laurel Dell, you might wish to examine them more closely. Ants are the most industrious creatures, it seems, moving for a few inches, hesitating, retreating, moving forward again, testing various green shoots with their feelers. The ants of the woodland are not the marching regiments of patio or house, but they do hurry on their way as if guided by a distinct purpose. They do not meander as we love to do.

From Laurel Dell the trail along the creek continues down Cataract Gulch to Alpine Lake (see Section 11). On the present walk, however, you should return to the south end of the meadow to pick up the *Mickey O'Brien Trail* to Barth's Retreat. The junction is well marked. From Barth's Retreat, you can pick up the *Laurel Dell Road*, which heads east to Potrero Camp. (You can also take this fire road from Laurel Dell—it leaves the meadow near the picnic tables—but it is not nearly so charming a route as the Mickey O'Brien Trail.) Before leaving Laurel Dell you might sit awhile by the creek, enjoying the hypnotic sounds of the water moving through the grass, the sight of the great laurels and maples, and the sense of serenity that pervades this special place.

The Mickey O'Brien Trail climbs alongside Barth's Creek for perhaps three-quarters of a mile, crossing a few side streams, climbing steeply for short distances here and there. At Barth's Retreat you will find a couple picnic tables, a metal grill, and a welcome drinking fountain. Nearby you can see picturesque Sargent cypresses (*Cupressus sargentii*) for the first time on this walk. A California endemic, this cypress is indigenous to only two areas in Marin County; you are in one of them. Follow the

wide dirt track to your left past one of these cypresses to the
Laurel Dell Road. Turn right and walk uphill a few steps to
a spectacular overlook. The northern part of Marin County
lies below you. To the west you can see Inverness Ridge
and the Pacific. To the northwest stretches the dark,
mountainous coast. The prominent peak in the northeast is
Mount St. Helena, at the head of the Napa Valley. To the
east San Pablo Bay sits placidly in the sun with the inner
Coast Ranges forming a hazy blue backdrop.

Near this view point you may see jack rabbits bound in
and out of the brush, or after a winter rain, deer tracks in the
muddy ruts of the road. The nearby gray-green serpentine,
which is inhospitable to most plants, hosts a tiny wildflower
that often prefers it to more fertile, well-watered areas. In
the spring you may see hundreds of tiny cerise and yellow
flowers, scarcely one inch tall and shaped something like
violets. But they are rather oddly shaped at that, and you
may not be able to find them in the average field guide. So
fragile that they look as if they will be gone in a week, these
flowers more resemble alpine miniatures than coastal
species. They are purple mouse ears (*Mimulus douglasii*), a
rather uncommon member of the same genus that includes
the abundant bush monkeyflower and the common yellow
monkeyflower. This large genus is represented in Marin
County by ten species. To the average observer the purple
mouse ears would seem unconnected with its more common
cousins because it lacks the distinctive snapdragon "chin"
common to the better known monkeyflowers.

You have emerged from the streamside woodland that
has characterized the hike up till now into the chaparral of
the serpentine barrens. In the spring, the sweet fragrance of
the ceanothus, which resembles a cross between jasmine

and lavender, rides on the breeze, attracting bee and hiker alike. Stop and inhale the heady sweetness of these blossoms and you will understand that they are not called wild lilac for their color alone.

The body of water far below and a little to your left is Alpine Lake, a man-made reservoir. Other reservoirs on the Marin water district lands are Bon Tempe, Lagunitas, and Phoenix lakes. An extensive system of trails and roads connects all of them with the cities that line the watershed, as well as with the higher slopes of Tamalpais itself. For the many possible routes in this watershed, consult the ''Freese Trail Map of the Mount Tamalpais Region,'' which is available in many bookstores and outdoor equipment shops in the Bay Area.

From the view point, head right (east) on the fire road, dropping downhill to a broad track leading left down to Potrero Meadows. Walk past the track for perhaps 50 yards to where an easily overlooked, unmarked foot path heads uphill on your right. Look for ''root steps'' and an old, uninformative signpost. This is the *Benstein Trail* back to Rock Springs. It moves uphill only a short distance, and this stretch is beautiful in a special way. Most of the steps are tree roots, and in between these steps are bits of rock, mostly green serpentine the color of jade. In some ways the Benstein Trail is reminiscent of a Japanese garden—perhaps it is the rock forms and the spaces around them or the varied and subtle colors and textures along the way.

As you climb higher, some of the rocks are enormous boulders, with nothing growing around them but various kinds of manzanita, which follow the forms of the rocks themselves. From time to time you may want to climb atop one of these boulders and sun yourself beside a lizard. You will know that you have reached the top when you see some fine old Sargent cypresses, which have that delicious Christmas-tree smell. You can recognize them by their dark foliage, picturesque shapes, flat, scaly needles, and small, knobby brown cones, which grow in clusters next to the branches. These ancient, gnarled trees make unforgettable frames for the view below.

Your climb ends here, and from now to the *Rock Springs-Lagunitas Road*, the Benstein Trail is a level path through a forest of tanoak, golden chinquapin, Douglas fir, and California laurel. There is a spot where the trail passes between two enormous Douglas firs, with just enough room for one person at a time to slip through. On your left is a fallen giant, a tanoak lost to storms and rains, whose base measures nine feet across and is split down the middle, as if by some supernatural ax. This tree was more than a hundred feet tall when it stood and supported twenty-three branches heavy enough to be called "trunks." They had fallen in a complete circle, like spokes of a wheel, taking down hundreds of branches from the trees around them.

The tanoak's botanical name, *Lithocarpus densiflora*, is derived from the Greek words *lithos*, meaning stone, and *karpos*, meaning fruit, the name referring to the extra hard shell of its fuzzy-capped acorns. Not a true oak, the tanoak is nevertheless a close relative. It can be recognized by its distinctive leaves—oblong and pointed, with prominent parallel veins that end in a small spike at the margin; the underside is paler green and covered with a yellowish down. The trunks of the tanoak are typically lighter gray than those of true oaks.

When the trail intersects the Rock Springs-Lagunitas Road, turn right and head up to Mountain Theater. One of the nice things about the road is that you can walk about three feet above it on a foot trail. Do not follow the sign on your right that says "Benstein Trail." This is a dense, closed-in stretch of the trail that winds back down to Laurel Dell. On your left you will pass a number of "woodpecker trees" that are worth a closer look. These dead Douglas firs, which stand out among the living, have been riddled by acorn woodpeckers, a rather large, very common woodpecker of the California oak woodlands. It drills the holes to store acorns for later use. Even telephone poles are not immune to this compulsive quartermaster. It also drills smaller holes in its search for insects. All along the road, "woodpecker trees" are used for lookouts by other birds.

You will meet the Ridgecrest Road just opposite the Mountain Theater parking area. To avoid even this short stretch of highway, take one of the paths leading off to your right from the Rock Springs-Lagunitas Road just as you first see the red gate that marks the junction with the highway. These cross each other over the grassy hills for about 300 feet to either Mountain Theater or the Rock Springs parking lot. If you have not seen Mountain Theater, you can cross the highway to the wooden stile and the paved path leading to the amphitheater. Built in the 1930s by the Civilian Conservation Corps, the theater was once the scene of frequent dramatic productions, some very good, others more distinguished by their enthusiasm than their acting. In recent years there have been no plays in the theater, but it is still used occasionally for large community events. Almost any time you will find people here and there, warming themselves on the serpentine seats, eating lunch, or simply admiring the staggering view.

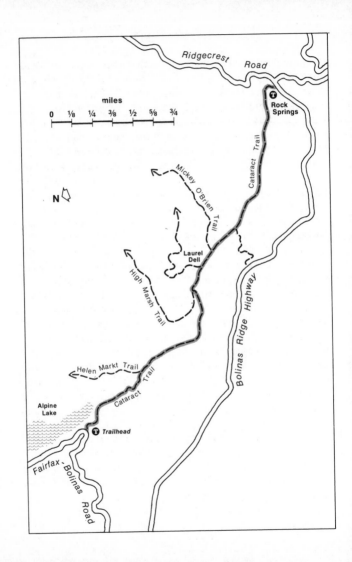

11. CATARACT GULCH

Some hikes on Mount Tamalpais are charming, others are spectacular. This one is both, combining the charm of a lush, wooded canyon, alive with ferns and moss and wildflowers, with the spectacle of roaring waterfalls dropping over massive boulders. It is also extremely steep, at times merely a stairway up the nearly vertical wall of the canyon, but this does not seem to stop people from making the trudge up to Laurel Dell from Alpine Lake, 854 feet below. If you have only one car, you have no way to avoid a stiff climb except by choosing another trail. But if you can arrange a shuttle, leaving one car at Alpine Lake and driving up to Rock Springs to begin your hike, you can enjoy the charm and spectacle of Cataract Gulch without much work at all. The total distance from Rock Springs to the trailhead at Alpine Lake is only about four miles. If a shuttle is impossible, it is best to begin your hike at Alpine Lake in order to get the steep climb out of the way first. Then, after a lunch or rest at Laurel Dell, you will have a leisurely walk back down the canyon. Although the canyon will be beautiful any time of the year, take this walk on a sunny day in winter or spring to see the falls at their best.

To get to the trailhead at Alpine Lake, take U.S. 101 north from San Francisco. Exit on Sir Francis Drake Boulevard; the sign over the exit itself directs you to San Anselmo. Drive west through Kentfield and Ross to "the Hub" in San Anselmo, a complicated intersection where you face two possible left turns. Either one will do in this case, but the first, hard left is preferable because it is prettier and more direct. You are now on Center Boulevard; follow it into Fairfax, where you turn left on the

Fairfax-Bolinas Highway (signed Bolinas Road here). After passing some stores, some homes, and a large country club and stables, this winding road strikes off through a picturesque landscape of woods and chaparral. In a few miles you will drop down to the shore of Alpine Lake. You can either park at the dam or if there is room, at the first hairpin turn after crossing over the dam. If you park at the dam, you must walk up the road to this turn in order to find the trailhead, which begins on the left at the turn.

Follow the trail along the south inlet of the lake, staying high and right at the first fork and low and left at the second. You will come to a sign reading, "Cataract Trail to Laurel Dell." After leaving the lake, you walk only a few hundred yards before encountering the first really steep stretch of trail. But there are immediate compensations. Not long after leaving the lake, look for an old fallen redwood across the streambed on your left. From this log grow no less than four younger redwoods, limbs or sprouts that made good when the old tree fell. These are not just saplings, but mature, though not ancient, trees. Two grow from the base of the log on the opposite bank; one from the middle, so that is is suspended above the stream; and one from the tip of the log on this side of the stream. This is one of the most striking examples of second-generation redwoods growing from a parent tree that you will find in the Bay Area. The tallest of the four scions must be eighty feet or so.

You will be in the company of redwoods only along this first portion of the trail. As it climbs, they are quickly replaced by Douglas firs, of which there are many fine old specimens in this canyon. As you walk through the forest of redwoods, big-leaf maple, madrone, and tanoak, the roar of the river grows louder and soon you get a glimpse of the first falls, a tall narrow shoot that plummets over a steep rock face, breaking into a series of cascades that tumble down the canyon to your very feet. This may well be the most impressive waterfall in the region.

You will certainly want to savor this falls at some length, for it is just here that the trail begins its first steep ascent, turning sharply right to begin the first of a series of switchbacks that climb steeply to a bench above the falls and to a second waterfall. To take your mind off the climb, admire the deep blue flowers of the Pacific houndstongue, which bloom abundantly along this stretch of trail. With them you will also find trillium, fetid adder's tongue, and the delicate white bouquets of the toothwort. But the special botanical treat of this climb lurks in the lush bank on your right as you complete the last switchback. For here, among the polypody ferns, which seem to be everywhere in this canyon, you will find the exquisite California maidenhair fern (*Adiantum jordani*), whose delicate palmate leaves are held aloft on stems of blackest wire.

At the top of this stretch you come to a charming footbridge over the creek. Made of rough-hewn beams, it has only one hand rail but is broad enough to pass over easily. Look upstream and you will see the second major waterfall on this creek, not so tall as the first but just as impressive in its own way. It falls over a sheer rock face in two streams, joined briefly at the top, then separated by a bold prominence of rock. Crossing the footbridge, you continue climbing on the other side of the creek to an even better vantage point for this waterfall.

Just above the bridge, you will come to a junction with the *Helen Markt Trail*; keep right. The Cataract Trail continues to climb steeply, levels out for a space, then climbs again to meet the stream, which for a while is far below. Just before the trail rounds a prominent exposed cliffside, at which point it is bordered by a stout metal guardrail, take an obvious footpath off to the right down to the stream. Here you face what is perhaps the most picturesque, indeed the most beautiful single spot in the Bay Area. A broad white sheet of foam, a bridalveil, streams down flat, polished gray rock, resolving itself at once into the stillness of a deep green pool. On the opposite side a hugh boulder festooned with moss and ferns rises steeply from the pool—a sheer wall of ferns waving over the water. Above it all, the dense, moist coastal forest; below you, its delicate grasses and blossoming herbs. This is a place to linger, a place you may not want to leave at all.

Most of the rest of the way up to Laurel Dell the trail is, if anything, steeper than it has been. Rock stairways are common along certain stretches. Though other short sections run level or only slightly uphill, these are mere intermissions in the slow steep stretch ahead. There is no hurry, of course; everywhere there are chances to learn more about the forest—to listen and look for birds, to examine the delicate beauty of wildflowers, to puzzle out the different species of ferns, or merely to sit by the stream.

Three wildflowers are especially evident along this trail in the spring. In the sunnier spots patches of grass are decorated in blue and yellow by the buttercup (*Ranunculus californicus*) and baby-blue-eyes (*Nemophila menziessi*), which are common and widespread throughout the Bay Area. Together, they make a striking display. Along the shady stretches of the trail—which is most of it—look for trillium, which bloom from January through April, with March probably the best month to see them. They are especially common along the Cataract Trail, some growing to good size. Though two species are found in Marin County, most hikers will encounter only the wake-robin (*Trillium ovatum*), for the common trillium (*Trillium chloropetalum*) is not really so common. Do not be misled, if you see a white trillium and a purple trillium, into necessarily believing you have seen both species. The petals of the wake-robin are white at first, but grow progressively pinker and darker as the flower ages. By the time they are ready to fall off, they may be nearly purple. The common trillium has either a red or greenish-white flower, but the best way to distinguish the two species is by the mottled leaves of the wake-robin, which the common trillium lacks.

As the trail continues its climb up Cataract Gulch, you will come to a junction with the *High Marsh Trail*. This heads northwest before turning east to traverse the north slope of Mt. Tam, linking up eventually with the *Kent Trail*, which can be taken north back to Alpine Lake. From here you can turn left on the Helen Markt Trail and continue until it meets the Cataract Trail just above the first falls. To go to Laurel Dell, keep right and keep climbing at the junction with the High Marsh Trail. You will pass one last waterfall, a long, steep cascade, really, plunging energetically through a narrow rock chute. If you do not mind scrambling down a steep bare slope, you can spend some time sitting on a large sunny boulder overlooking this white water. From this point you make the last short climb to Laurel Dell, emerging suddenly out of both woods and canyon into a large grassy meadow. From here you can either continue up to Rock Springs or turn around and head back down after a suitable rest. During the spring Laurel Dell puts on a fine show of wildflowers.

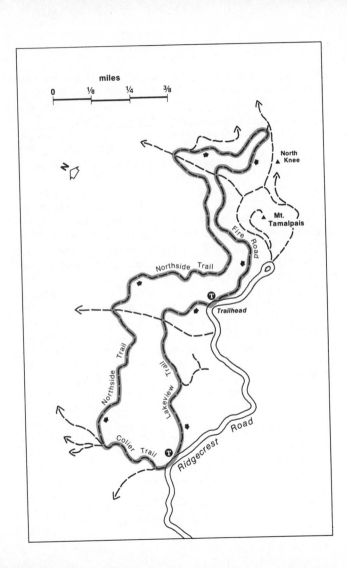

12. NORTHSIDE TRAIL

The *Northside Trail* explores one of the least-visited areas on Mount Tamalpais, making it an ideal choice for a warm, crowded weekend. Traversing the steep northern slope of East Peak—the summit of Tamalpais—the trail runs nearly level from Inspiration Point to Collier Spring, a distance of just over one and a half miles. But hikers must be prepared to make a steep descent down to the trail and a steep climb back up, which may explain why so few people seem to use it. Certainly there is no other good reason, for the Northside Trail offers superlative views, an abundance of spring wildflowers, an interesting variety of flora and vegetation, and two bubbling springs set in redwood groves.

This is not the trail to choose for a casual family outing, but it should present no problem to the average hiker who doesn't mind a bit of steep switchbacking. Heavy-soled boots are recommended for this hike and are absolutely necessary if you elect to take the steep route down from North Shoulder. But there are easier routes for those who wish to attempt the hike in good walking shoes. Although there is a spring along the way, you should carry your own water. Since this hike can be made in a morning or afternoon, you need not bring a lunch, although there are several good spots for picnicking along the way.

The ideal time to make this hike would be at daybreak on a warm day in early spring. The seasonal streams would still be running, the wildflowers would already be blooming, and you could watch the sun come up over the bay. Perhaps the worst time would be in late summer or early fall, when the streams are dry and the weather hot. Much of this route goes through open country, so the sun can become a little oppressive on a windless day. But despite this advice, you will still find the trail perfectly acceptable in hot weather, *provided you wear a hat and sunglasses and carry a good supply of water*.

From San Francisco, drive north on U.S. 101 to the Mill Valley/Stinson Beach exit. Head west on state highway 1—the Shoreline Highway—to a traffic signal about a half mile from the freeway. Turn left at the signal and drive for about three miles to the junction with Panoramic Highway. Take the right fork and drive up Mount Tamalpais, passing Mountain Home in two and a half miles, Bootjack Camp in about five miles, and coming to the junction with Southside Road at Pan Toll in five and one-third miles. Turn right and follow winding Southside Road to Rock Springs, where you turn right on Ridge Crest Road. Drive for one and two-thirds miles to the saddle between Middle Peak and East Peak. There is a dirt turn-out on the right. The *Collier Trail* takes off just across the highway, switchbacking steeply down to Collier Spring, where you pick up the Northside Trail and head east. The Collier Trail drops 425 feet in just over a quarter mile, switchbacking relentlessly down through sparse woods that gradually grow lusher as you approach the redwoods lining the middle fork of Lagunitas Creek.

There are three alternatives to going down the Collier Trail. For all of them, drive to the parking lot just below East Peak. The first and, for most people, the best route down to the Northside Trail is the fire road that leaves Ridge Crest Road just beyond the west end of the parking lot. Park your car as close as you can to the point where the road separates into two one-way roads. Walk downhill along the road until you see a fire road leading off to the right. This winds around the north slope of the mountain. In about a half mile it meets the *East Peak Fire Trail*, which drops in a steep hot swath to Inspiration Point and the Northside Trail. For a more leisurely route, ignore the East Peak Fire Trail and continue on the road for another third of a mile, where it meets the Northside Trail just a few hundred yards east of Inspiration Point. This junction is signed; you turn left off the fire road.

The second alternative to the Collier Trail is the most adventuresome. Take the *Verna Dunshee Trail*, which begins near the restrooms at the east end of the parking lot. Head downhill to your right; a sign marks the beginning of this paved walk around East Peak. This route offers incredible views of San Francisco, the ocean, the bay, and southern Marin County. To the east lie the Berkeley hills, and beyond them the massive, double-crowned summit of Mount Diablo. This is the dawn trail, if you decide to come that early. After passing a lookout point (which here seems redundant), crossing a wooden bridge, and winding among huge, picturesque rock outcroppings, you will come to the *Temelpa Trail*, which heads downhill on your right. Pass it up and continue on the paved trail until you are just below the prominent "needle" rock on your left. Here a trail heads out through the low scrub to the point known as North Shoulder, which is clearly visible a short way to the east.

From North Shoulder a trail of sorts drops like a rock down the precipitous eastern face of the mountain. It joins the fire road winding down from Ridge Crest Road (first alternative above) in about a third of a mile. Here the fire road makes a hairpin turn; take the lower arm of the turn and walk for a third of a mile to the junction with the Northside Trail. *CAUTION: do not attempt the route down from North Shoulder unless you have some experience in steep rock scrambling and are wearing heavy-soled boots. This is not a route for families or the casual weekend walker.*

The third alternative is perhaps the least attractive of all the possible routes down to the Northside Trail. It is steep without being adventuresome. From the restrooms at the east end of the parking lot, two broad tracks take off on your left as you face east. (The upper track climbs to the summit of East Peak, a good side trip for another day.) Follow the lower track around the west and north sides of the mountain until you come to the *East Peak Fire Trail*. This unattractive route descends *very steeply* to the fire road coming down from Ridge Crest Road. Here you can either continue down to Inspiration Point or, if you've had enough, turn right on the fire road for a more reasonable, if more circuitous, route to the same place.

But for most people, the best way to begin this hike is to walk down to Collier Spring. From the dirt turn-out in the saddle between East and Middle Peaks, cross the road and bear slightly left along the oppsoite shoulder until you see a narrow, unmarked trail heading downhill through the trees in a westerly direction. Take this path and you will shortly come to a trail heading off on your right. This is the Collier Trail, and you should turn right at this junction. (The trail continuing straight ahead is the *International Trail*.) On your way down to Collier Spring, you will cross several faint paths, any one of which could be confusing. In each case, follow the more obvious path. But toward the bottom of this climb, not too far before you come to Collier Spring, you will encounter a junction similar to the one with the International Trail, where your route suddenly departs from what would seem to be the trail. Here, too, you should turn right. Remember that this trail switchbacks down the slope, so beware of any long, easy traverses; they probably mean you have missed a turn.

You begin this steep descent in dry, open, scrubby woodlands that grow lusher as you approach Collier Spring. The upper parts of the trail are dominated by oaks, bays, and a few scrawny California nutmegs. Soon you begin to see more madrones and a few Douglas firs. Finally, as the trail drops down alongside Lagunitas Creek, you enter deep redwoods. Collier Spring is a delightful place to rest a few minutes from the steep switchbacks you have just completed. It is located in a fine grove of redwoods, and you will find a log bench set up right beside he small stream that issues forth from the spring.

Four trails intersect at Collier Spring; the junctions are well posted. As you face downstream, the first trail to your left is the *Upper Northside Trail*, which heads west to Rifle Camp and Potrero Meadows. The obvious fork off this trail to the right is the *Lower Northside Trail*, which meets the *Berry Trail* down to Bon Tempe Lake at the Rock Springs-Lagunitas Road. Straight ahead, the Collier Trail continues down the canyon, paralleling the stream all the way to Lake Lagunitas. To the right the Northside Trail heads east to Inspiration Point. This is your route.

As you leave Lagunitas Creek, you leave the redwoods. The forest becomes drier, more open, and dominated by oaks, California laurels, tanoaks, and madrones—the typical species of the coastal mixed-evergreen woodland. Here and there a Douglas fir towers over the broad-crowned trees. But within a quarter mile, you enter a second grove of redwoods and come to your second mountain spring. This delightful seep bubbles from the ground right at the trail, and with the stately redwoods overhead combines to make this an especially charming spot. The trees here are second-growth for the most part, lacking the size and conspicuous fire scars of older redwoods. There are, however, one or two older specimens in this grove, including one leaning way over. There must be ample groundwater here—as, indeed, the spring suggests—for these redwoods march down the open north slope as if it were a damp, cool, foggy coastal canyon. You will notice that elsewhere along this trail there are no groves such as this. We have the small spring to thank for these splendid trees.

Before leaving the spring, look downhill through the grove, where you will see a tree with gray rather than reddish-brown bark. It is just about as tall and big around as the redwoods, but it is a California laurel, normally a broad-crowned tree, which has imitated the redwoods as the only way of competing for sunlight. Although the sight of a laurel straining upwards in a redwood grove is a common one, this particular tree seems to have been especially successful and surely must be one of the most remarkable examples of this phenomenon in the Bay Area.

From the spring and the grove, the Northside Trail traverses the slope for perhaps a quarter mile to the ridge separating the middle and east forks of Lagunitas Creek. Here it meets the *Lagunitas Fire Trail*, an extremely steep path linking Ridge Crest Road to Lake Lagunitas. Keep straight ahead, reentering woods as you drop down from the crest of the ridge.

During the spring you will pass fabulous displays of iris at various points along this trail. They grow in profusion along the damper—though not necessarily wet—stretches.

The orchidlike flowers may be blue, lavender, purple, cream, or white. Other wildflowers to look for include the star lily, buttercups, lupine, Pacific houndstongue, Indian paintbrush, and Indian warrior. This last flower, like the paintbrush, is a member of the large figwort family, which includes such other springtime favorites as monkeyflowers, penstemon, and snapdragons. The Indian warrior typically is found in partial shade along the trail. It somewhat resembles paintbrush but its leaves are lacier and its flower is burgundy rather than scarlet. It is also common along many other Tamalpais trails.

The views from the more open stretches of this trail are spectacular. Far to the west stretch the hills of Marin, some densely wooded with redwood and Douglas fir, others covered with grass and scrub, with only scattered patches and fingers of oak woodlands breaking the smooth, undulating ridges. Directly below you lie Bon Tempe Lake and Lake Lagunitas, two reservoirs of the Marin Municipal Water District. Lagunitas is the smaller lake closer to you. On a clear day you can see the hills of Sonoma and Napa counties far to the north. The highest peak in the northeast is Mount St. Helena.

After leaving the Lagunitas Fire Trail, the Northside Trail gradually veers toward the south as it enters the canyon of the east fork of Lagunitas Creek. The stream proper begins farther down the canyon. Up here, just below the crest of the mountain, you cross only a few small tributaries, which are dry from shortly after the last rain in spring to the first rain the following autumn. Nevertheless, there is moisture enough in this canyon to support a dense woodland, including big-leaf maple, which generally favors moist sites. This is the last good place to rest and eat lunch. From here the hike gets hotter and the woods sparser.

The Northside Trail traverses the east slope of the canyon for about a half mile before meeting the East Peak Fire Trail at Inspiration Point. Just why this particular spot should merit the name is a mystery: it is no more inspirational than any other spot along this trail, and in some ways it is far less attractive. It is a hot, exposed place that is made even less inspirational by the wide orange swath of the East Peak Fire Trail, which heads directly up the mountain. Although this dirt road will get you up to Ridge Crest Road, pass it up for the gentler, cooler, more scenic route that heads off into the woods directly across the clearing.

You are now on the last, short leg of the Northside Trail. Shortly you will come to a dirt road. This is the fire road leading up to Ridge Crest Road just below the East Peak parking lot. It parallels the slope through increasingly sparse woodlands, meeting the North Shoulder route in about a quarter of a mile. Here the woods give way to chaparral. The North Shoulder route is a hot, treacherous, fiercely steep, and unnecessary climb even for a strong, experienced hiker. It is not steep enough to be a real challenge, but just steep enough to completely exhaust you. So follow the road around the hairpin turn and climb moderately up to Ridge Crest Road.

(If you make this hike by coming down this road, you may have trouble finding the continuation of Northside Trail at Inspiration Point. Walk directly across the clearing and look for a narrow, unmarked path leading down through the scrub. This is the trail.)

From Ridge Crest Road you have two choices for getting back to your car. You can either walk for a mile along the highway, which is possible though not advisable since the shoulders are narrow and the traffic heavy, or you can pick up the *Lake View Trail*, which heads off to the right a few yards west of the fire road. This old dirt road merely parallels the Northside Trail, though a couple of hundred feet above it, winding around a shoulder to meet the Lagunitas Fire Trail, which you crossed below on the Northside Trail. Continue on the road until you see a path leading off to the right just where the road makes a sharp turn to the left. This trace heads out to Lakeview Point, which is directly above the small spring set in the redwood grove on the Northside Trail. From here, the trail continues another quarter mile to Ridge Crest Road, emerging out of the woods just a few yards east of the Collier Trail.

If you began the hike at the East Peak parking lot, taking the Northside Trail west to Collier Spring and the Collier Trail up to the highway, you can find the trail to Lakeview Point by walking along the north side of the highway until you see a narrow path heading off into the woods. It is unmarked, but offers a better way back to the parking lot than the road. The total loop is about four miles.

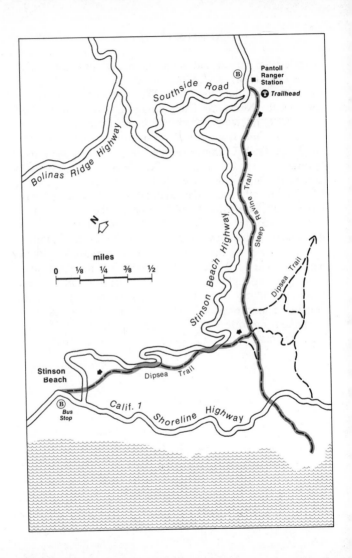

13. STEEP RAVINE

For many people, the walk down Steep Ravine, from Pan Toll to Stinson Beach, is the best trail on Mount Tamalpais because it combines the fun of waterfalls with the rain-forest quality of big redwoods, winding up at last in the open hills above the sea. Steep Ravine is most dramatic after a winter storm or in the early spring, when Webb's Creek, at its fullest, becomes a cataract, when the moss and ferns are most luxurious. Tennis shoes or other walking shoes are fine, though you might appreciate an extra pair of socks if the path has been recently rained on. Remember to bring a lunch to eat beside the biggest falls.

The best way to make this walk is to arrange a car shuttle. Leave one car at Stinson Beach and drive in a second car to Pan Toll. There is a fee of $1.00 to park in the lot by the ranger station. If you cannot make shuttle arrangements, you can ride the 62 (Bolinas) bus back up to Pan Toll; it leaves Stinson Beach at regular intervals every day of the week. Consult the Golden Gate Transit District for exact schedules.

From San Francisco, drive north on U.S. 101 to the Mill Valley/Stinson Beach exit. Turn left at the first stop sign and drive about half a mile to an intersection with a stop light. Turn left; in about three miles you will come to the junction with Panoramic Highway. If you plan to take the bus back up the mountain, turn left and drive up to Pan Toll. If you have arranged a shuttle, keep left on the Shoreline Highway, which winds down through Green Gulch to Muir Beach, climbs up over the coastal ridge, and drops down to the other side, hugging the steep cliff most of the way to Stinson Beach. Park in town along the main street. Take the second car and head back the way you came to the Stinson Beach Highway, which heads uphill on your left just outside of town. Follow this road all the way to Pan Toll. Bus service is available to Mountain Home, Bootjack Camp, and Pan Toll. Take the 62 (Bolinas) bus from the East Bay Terminal, at Fremont and Mission in San Francisco. For other stops in the city, and for exact schedules, call 332-6600.

Take the middle trail, marked "Steep Ravine," from the west end of the parking lot. The trail leads off through Douglas firs and California laurels to a series of well-made switchbacks. The steps, bridges, handrails, and ladder make this an easy downhill walk from an elevation of about 1,200 feet to sea level. The total distance to Stinson Beach is about three miles.

Between winter storms, this walk becomes a spectacular journey as the rains dump torrents of water into Webb Creek, turning this pleasant little stream into a splendid series of waterfalls. It is a nice coincidence that just when the jangling noise of the holidays has wound up your nervous system, the weatherman will toss in a sparkling sunny day when you can take to the mountain. In the summer, when the creek is not so wild and noisy, the first part of the trail is filled with the constant quarreling of scrub jays and squirrels, who make off with tidbits from the nearby campground.

Just past the first bench, in sight of the creek, you enter the redwood forest, whose accustomed serenity is interrupted in winter by the joyous roar of water, as stream after stream spills over both sides of the ravine, making miniature waterfalls that are but the first contributions to the growing torrent you follow all the way to the *Dipsea Trail*.

The distinctive smell of wet redwoods, the special spongy feel of centuries of forest compost, and the odd delight at suddenly becoming a miniature human in a giant's forest—all these senstaions combine to take you back into another, much earlier world. Every turn in the trail reveals a new stream splashing and crashing over the rocks. As you pause by the stream, take a closer look at the ferns.

The big, coarse-leaved ferns that form fountain-like sprays along the stream are sword ferns (*Polystichum munitum*). These stay green all winter, but some species, like the western bracken (*Pteridium aquilinum*), die back during the wet season and then return each spring by sending up dozens of new fiddle-neck fronds all at once. Their lacy fronds provide a striking contrast to the giant horsetail (*Equisetum telmateia*) you will also find, which looks something like Egyptian papyrus. This primitive inhabitant of bogs and streamsides belongs to a family that dates back to the Pennsylvanian Period, some 200 million years ago.

One of the more interesting ferns in Steep Ravine is the California polypody (*Polypodium californicum*), whose leaflets are rounded at the tips, as if an artist had drawn them with a long, easy scribble. The polypodys are smaller than the sword ferns, which they resemble, and tend to grow in little colonies. Occasionally, you will see two other species of polypody. One, the leather fern (*Polypodium scouleri*), is easily recognized by the decidedly long "nose" at the end of each frond. The other, known as the licorice fern (*Polypodium glycyrrhiza*), is to be found in little pockets tucked away in rocks or logs. Its leaflets grow in a staggered fashion, rather than opposite each other, and have small points on their tips. If you pinch one of the fronds, your fingers will retain the licoricelike fragrance. You may also discover the elegant maidenhair fern (*Adiantum jordani*) moving ever so slightly on its wirelike black stems, or the golden-back fern (*Pityrogramma triangulanis*), which leaves a powdery golden stipple when you press a frond against the back of your hand.

Children especially enjoy the golden-back fern, but not nearly so much as they do that common monster of the coastal forest, the banana slug, which reaches an impressive four inches of banana-shaped length. Eating its way through the moist green salads of the undergrowth, a more harmless monster would be hard to find. Yet these long yellow-green slugs, which have a way of lying about the trail, can give quite a start to someone who has never encountered them before.

The most unusual feature of the *Steep Ravine Trail* is the ladder that drops down the biggest boulder along the trail. Built by the Civilian Conservation Corps during the thirties, this ladder is quaint but necessary. From the top of the boulder, you look down over a waterfall and pool. This is a good place for one—and only one—person to eat lunch, though the redwood log at the base of the boulder will accommodate a companion. If you prefer a drier, more spacious site for a picnic, continue for another 500 feet, crossing still another bridge to reach a series of waterfalls and a round pool, which itself has a fall of foam from its lip to an even deeper pool below. This is a splendid place to rest.

The redwoods in Steep Ravine may be first-growth trees, though not so ancient as those of Muir Woods. They seem like it, anyway. For one thing, you find no stumps, the usual signs of a logged-off forest. For another, fire has blackened the older trees, whose fluted trunks spiral upward. Younger trees seldom show such extensive scars because they would probably not survive the fire. The ravine is so steep that perhaps in the early days it was simply not worth the trouble and expense to go after these trees. When you approach the junction with the Dipsea Trail, you will begin to see evidence of some logging in this flatter, more open area.

When you reach the Dipsea Trail, you have three alternatives, besides turning around and heading back up the way you came.

One is to take the Dipsea Trail to the left; it heads east, back toward Muir Woods. In about a mile and a half, you would come to the *T.C.C. Trail*, where you would turn left and walk for about a third of a mile to pick up the short, steep *Stapelveldt Trail* up to Pan Toll.

Your second alternative is to continue down the Steep Ravine Trail to Shoreline Highway and across the highway to the bluffs overlooking the sea. This alternative is advisable only if you have a car waiting nearby on the highway.

The third alternative, and the one taken by most people, is to turn right on the Dipsea Trail and walk to the town of Stinson Beach. The trail winds past black angus cows down into a gully of willows and laurels, joining and leaving the Stinson Beach Highway on its way down the mountain. In the winter, when the gully is wet, you might prefer to take the road all the way into Stinson Beach, for this part of the trail can be a mass of fertile-smelling mud. If the day is warm you may want to spend some time at Stinson Beach basking in the sun before making the trip back up to Pan Toll.

14. MATT DAVIS TRAIL TO STINSON BEACH

From the 2,571-foot summit of Mount Tamalpais a gentle ridge dips toward the west, losing only 600 feet in a little over two and a half miles. Then, in a final mile or so, it plunges 2,000 feet to the sea. From Pan Toll, the *Matt Davis Trail* winds down 1,200 feet of this precipitous western face of the mountain, offering the hiker breathtaking views of San Francisco, the Pacific Ocean, and the Inverness Ridge. The trail is three and one-half miles long and easy going most of the way. Only in the final mile or so, when the trail switchbacks very steeply down into the heavily wooded canyon of Table Rock Creek, will the average hiker encounter any difficulty. Because of the sometimes treacherous footing on this final stretch, heavy-soled hiking boots are advisable, but with care and patience you will find good walking shoes acceptable. Dress warmly if it is windy.

Unless you relish the huff and puff of an exceptionally steep climb, begin this walk at Pan Toll rather than Stinson Beach. You can avoid the walk back up by arranging a car shuttle; leave one car at Stinson Beach and take the other up to Pan Toll. There is a fee of $1.00 to leave your car in the parking lot at the ranger station. If you can't make arrangements for a shuttle, you can ride the bus back up to Pan Toll; it leaves Stinson Beach at regular intervals every day of the week. Consult the Golden Gate Transit District for exact schedules.

From San Francisco, drive north on U.S. 101 to the Mill Valley/Stinson Beach exit. Turn left at the first stop sign and drive about a half mile to an intersection with a

stoplight. Turn left; you are on the Shoreline Highway (state route 1). In about three miles you will come to the junction with Panoramic Highway, which forks off to the right. If you plan to take the bus back up the mountain, turn right and drive to Pan Toll. If you have arranged a shuttle, keep left on the Shoreline Highway, which winds down through Green Gulch to Muir Beach, climbs up over the coastal ridge, and drops down to the other side, hugging the steep cliff most of the way to Stinson Beach. Just before entering the town, turn right on the Stinson Beach Highway. Just past the first hairpin turn in the road, park on the large dirt turn-out on your right. Take the second car and continue up the road to Pan Toll. Bus service is available to Mountain Home, Bootjack Camp, and Pan Toll. Take the 62 (Bolinas) bus from the East Bay Terminal, at Fremont and Mission in San Francisco. For other stops in the city, and for exact schedules, call 332-6600.

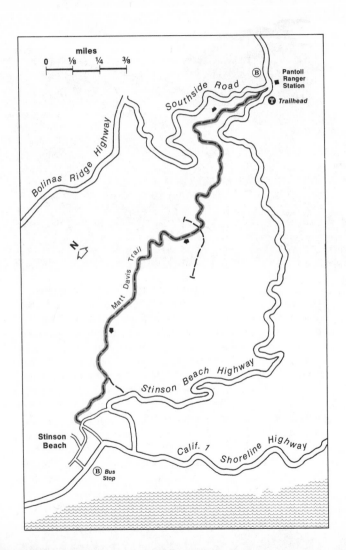

From the parking lot at Pan Toll, cross the highway and scramble up the bank on the other side to a signpost reading ''Matt Davis Trail, No Dogs.'' This is the trailhead. From here you get a preview of the magnificent views that characterize this trail. You can see San Francisco to the south and the open Pacific to the west, both prospects framed by wooded knolls. From here to Stinson Beach the trail is virtually all downhill, so you shouldn't be too tired at the end of the walk, though your legs may feel the effects of putting on the brakes during the final steep descent. Along the way you will discover many delightful places to picnic, soak up the sun, or drink in the breathtaking views that surround you.

From the trailhead you walk briefly through grass and shrubs, accented here and there by serpentine outcrops, before entering the deep woods of Douglas fir, laurel, and tanoak. The trail along this stretch is a delight to walk on, being soft forest duff and for the most part excellently engineered. It traverses the slope of the canyon drained by Webb Creek, winding up one side and back out the other before crossing a ridge and emerging into open grasslands. Along the way you cross lovely streams cascading over exposed serpentine, each of them so picturesque that you are tempted to rest awhile even though you have barely started your hike.

You will discover more easily the creamy white flowers of the star lily and the bright blue blossoms of the houndstongue, both of which are common to the forests of Mt. Tam. A particularly showy flower to be found along the less shady stretches of the trail is the red larkspur (*Delphinium nudicaule*). A single plant will have several flowers, each growing singly at the end of a long stem. The flowers resemble little hammerheads or perhaps an odd-looking fellow wearing a dwarf's cap. The long red "spur" extending back from the petals accounts for both of these similes. The petals themselves are partly yellow. Related to the garden delphinium, the red larkspur has been cultivated in English gardens since 1870. It is widespread in Marin County.

Look for giant chain ferns in the stream bottoms and small polypody ferns on the hillsides. Later on this hike, you will walk through lovely gardens of sword ferns, mass plantings as it were, giving the forest the look and feel of a tropical jungle. Along this first part of the walk, after you have crossed the footbridge over Webb Creek, you will notice the archway of California laurels, forming a bower over the trail. A Douglas fir, uprooted no doubt by a storm, has toppled over on to the more slender trees below and bent them over. There are many toppled trees along this stretch, which bear witness to the ferocity of winter winds on this mountain even in protected canyons such as this. Where the laurels have not been so forcibly constrained, the limitations of light and their need to compete with the taller Douglas firs have led them to assume grotesque shapes of various sorts. Many of them look like they should be growing in some enchanted forest or fairyland.

About a mile from the trailhead you leave the woods and begin to walk on a broad grassy knoll, which in the spring is thick with buttercups and lupine. The view spread out before you to the south and west is, frankly, awesome. From here, the mountain falls away so steeply to the west that you almost seem to be peering over the edge. On a clear day you can easily pick out many of the major landmarks in San Francisco to the south. From this angle the ocean is one immense spangled sheet. Yet despite the openness of the landscape and the immensity of the view, you do not feel exposed here, as, for example, you do sometimes on the rolling downs of Point Reyes. These grasslands are somehow more intimate, perhaps because they are relieved here and there by dark groves of Douglas fir and goldcup oak. And of course, there is something in man that loves a lawn, especially when it is decked with flowers and overlooks a magnificent view. Hikers in the high country of the Sierra will recognize here a charm not unlike that of the alpine gardens nestled in the barren granite of the peaks—both command spectacular, exhilarating vistas and at the same time feel cozy. Except on windy days, these grassy uplands demand that you tarry, whether to eat lunch or merely to lie in the sun.

Continuing along the trail through the grasslands, you will soon come to a stock fence and a stile for hikers. If you have given in to the temptation to drink from the streams before this point, don't do so hereafter, for you can expect to see cattle in the meadows. The trail winds around to a low saddle, from which you have a new and equally spectacular view, this time straight down—it seems—to Bolinas Lagoon and Inverness Ridge. You can see Point Reyes itself in the distance. Soon you will cross a trace, which, in both directions, leads nowhere. You might as well make your own trails over the open hills as follow this curious path. So keep straight ahead, passing a post with an arrow meant to keep you on the path. But before leaving this saddle, turn around and look to the east. From here you can see San Francisco, one tower of the Golden Gate Bridge, and far away on the horizon, the prominent summit of Mount Diablo.

From the saddle the trail winds through grasslands, then into a wooded canyon, where you must climb over a fence, then more grasslands, followed by a second canyon. When you emerge into the open, it will be for the last time until you make the final brief descent to your car. So if you have not yet had your fill of sun, rest here awhile. There are good sheltered spots to eat lunch at the forest's edge, should you need to escape from the wind.

Several species of birds seem to prefer these grassy "balds" on the coastal hills, and if you sit in one place long enough, you are sure to see the western bluebird, robin, and pink-sided junco. Vultures and red-tailed hawks are commonly sighted overhead, riding the thermals that shoot up this steep western face of the mountain. The male western bluebird is a jewel, but you will probably need field glasses to appreciate his splendor. In the right light his wings and back shine with the richest royal blue. Unlike the eastern bluebird, the western bluebird also has a pale blue bib extending from the head down on the upper part of the breast. This is one of the few songbirds that hovers on the wind like a hawk as it scans the grasses for insects. Upon finding one, it will suddenly swoop to the catch, only to resume its hovering minutes later.

Upon entering the woods, the trail immediately becomes steeper, winding down through tall Douglas firs, with an understory of huckleberries and tanoak. Soon it becomes steep enough to require switchbacks. This is the beginning of the long steep descent into the canyon of Table Rock Creek, which empties into Bolinas Lagoon just above Stinson Beach. From here on the trail gets progressively rougher. At times, it is little more then a crudely built stairway over roots and rocks, treacherous footing at best and the one place where you might want heavy-soled boots. But even here good walking shoes will get you by if you are careful enough. There are plenty of handholds to steady you over the rougher stretches, but until the trail finally clears out toward the bottom of the canyon be extremely careful about how you pick up and where you put down your feet.

On your way down, you will come to two junctions. The first, near the first mass of sword ferns, is marked with a post. Follow the arrow to the left. The second comes just before the trail begins the steep series of switchbacks. Keep right. After you have negotiated the roughest part of the trail, it levels out just above Table Rock Creek, a vigorous stream that reminds you of similar creeks in the Sierra or other high mountain ranges. The trail follows the stream for a short distance to Table Rock, a broad flat seat in the sun with a splendid view of Stinson Beach and Bolinas. Approach the edge of the rock with extreme caution because it drops off abruptly for at least fifty feet, if not more. This rock is like a platform in the forest because, with the land dropping away as it does, you look down on many trees. Except when a strong wind is blowing up the canyon from the Pacific, this is an ideal spot for lunch so long as you have your own beverage, be it water or wine or whatever. There is no water nearby. From the rock, you can pick out at least five species of trees—Douglas firs, California laurels, oaks, white alders, and California buckeye, which are especially common here. The buckeye (*Aesculus californicus*), with its bright green compound leaves and, in the late spring, its showy spikes of white bloom, is more typical of the drier hills farther inland than it is of a coastal canyon such as this one. But its presence here can be no accident. The factors that determine which plants grow where are complex and only imperfectly understood, but we can be sure that some combination of soil, exposure, moisture, and similar factors have made it perfectly at home in the woods of Table Rock.

From the rock you are only ten minutes or so from your car, though the descent to the road is extremely steep. A maze of trails seem to lead from the rock. The one on the right takes you to Stinson Beach near the fire house (also a reasonable place to leave a second car) and is your choice if you plan to take the bus back up to Pan Toll. If you parked your car on the Stinson Beach highway, take the "middle" trail, which is easily the most obvious path of the lot. This leads abruptly out of the woods into a steep open hillside covered with coastal scrub, especially coast sagebrush and bush lupine. The path drops like an elevator, so be very careful as you make your way down. You may find that the grass provides better footholds for the descent than the trail itself. At the bottom, you will pass through an overgrown boggy area where you should be especially careful of poison oak, which everywhere threatens to take over the path. A safe passage is usually possible, but only if you are forewarned of the danger. Just before the highway you will have to leap or wade through a brief wet muddy patch, but it is no real obstacle. Your car is waiting to the left a few yards up the road.

15. STINSON BEACH

North of Point Conception the California coast is not particularly hospitable to swimmers and sunbathers. The ocean is cold and treacherous all year round; the summers are cool and foggy; winds are strong and perennial; sand beaches are the exception rather than the rule. Nevertheless, there are some fine exceptions, and one of the finest is Stinson Beach, which lies at the very foot of the western slope of Mount Tamalpais. Although it too has its share of foggy and windy days, it also enjoys some protection from the elements. This is provided by the headlands of Bolinas, which comprise the southernmost tip of the Point Reyes Peninsula. These headlands cut some of the fog and wind, gentle the waters, and account in large part for the very existence of the beach. The prevailing currents along this coast run from north to south, but where countercurrents are set up (by headlands, for example), sands from down-current cliffs may be swept northward along the shore to form beaches and spits. Thus did Limantour Spit form behind Point Reyes and Stinson Beach behind the Bolinas headlands.

Of the beaches in the Bay Area that provide all the things necessary to a good old-fashioned family outing, Stinson is probably the most protected. Since almost everyone seems to appreciate this advantage, it is also one of the most popular beaches. Yet even though it is invariably crowded on warm weekends and holidays, it is big enough so that you can escape most of the people if you wish. It is a fine, clean strand about three miles long. On the south it ends at the foot of steep cliffs; from there it extends to the mouth of Bolinas Lagoon, forming a narrow sandspit for the last mile

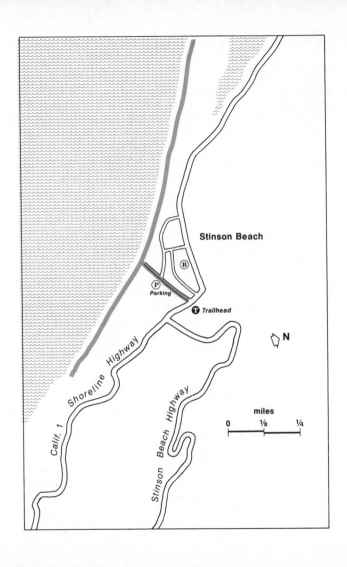

or so. The hike to the spit's end is an enjoyable one. For real solitude, walk this beach on a weekday or during weather when sunbathers stay away. On the other hand, if you want to enjoy a typical American seashore scene—weenie roasts, football games in the sand, kids splashing in the surf— Stinson is a fine place for that as well.

Stinson Beach is also a good place to rest up after hiking down to the coast from Pan Toll, up on Mt. Tam (see Sections 13 and 14). You can polish off a hike by taking your boots off and lying in the sun. If you are waiting for a bus to take you back up the mountain to your car, what could be better than a warm beach?

From San Francisco, drive north on U.S. 101 to the Mill Valley/Stinson Beach exit (Highway 1). Drive a half mile to a traffic light and turn left. In about three miles you come to the junction with Panoramic Highway, which heads up Mount Tamalpais. Keep right, following the sign directing you to the town of Stinson Beach. For a nominal fee you can park in the lot at Stinson Beach State Park, or if you can find room, on the main street of the town. It is only a short walk to the beach from Highway 1. Bus service is available to Stinson Beach. Take the 62 (Bolinas) bus from the East Bay Terminal, at Fremont and Mission in San Francisco. For other stops in the city, and for exact schedules, call 332-6600. There are dressing rooms, snack bars, picnic tables and grills among the trees that line the beach, and one of the broadest, longest white-sand beaches in the Bay Area. The strand is often sheltered from the prevailing northwest winds by the distant Inverness Ridge. Directly behind the beach, the steep western slope of Mt. Tam offers sunbathers a magnificent view of forest and grasslands. The long sand spit at the north end of the state park has something for everyone—except for the family dog, who is unwelcome along the entire beach. The rule against dogs is strictly enforced.

The village of Stinson Beach offers a variety of basic services, but it is not a typical seashore tourist trap. The mood here is low-key, and there is a bookstore with a good selection of natural history guides near the beach. The official entrance to the state park is just a few hundred feet north of the main intersection in town. Parking is ample, even on the most crowded days. Or you can walk toward the beach from the intersection, passing through a gate next to a hot dog stand, across a footbridge, and through the picnic grounds to the beach. The dressing rooms are well kept, and lifeguards are on duty during the summer and on holidays.

The beach is great for all things that Americans have traditionally enjoyed—beachballs, sand castles, picnics, or just lying around. It is a great place for people watching, or if you prefer birds, you can turn over and watch the pelicans passing single file over the edge of the breaking surf. Stinson Beach is a very clean beach—not one for shells or sea life. Not many people swim in the ocean off northern California because the waters, at best, warm up only to the tolerable side of frigid. But for those who like their swims brisk, by October the sun has made the ocean here as warm as it will ever be. Almost nobody ventures into the surf—at least not without a wet suit—in spring or early summer.

But of the Bay Area beaches, which tend to have treacherous currents and riptides, Stinson Beach is among the safest. It surely is the safest of those with real surf. If you can take the water, you can wade out or ride the waves in relative safety. After a swim or lunch, or if you simply want to walk, you can either head north along the sandspit or south toward the cliffs and rocks.

16. AUDUBON CANYON RANCH

The Audubon Canyon Ranch provides a unique opportunity to observe the great blue heron and great egret as they raise their young in huge stick nests built on the very tops of redwood trees. The canyon opens on the Bolinas Lagoon, where the birds feed. If one were to use a single word to describe the "ranch," it would be "harmony," for here in this tranquil rural setting there is an almost perfect balance between man and the land. The largest and one of the last major egret and heron rookeries on the coast, Audubon Canyon Ranch is a perfect outdoor laboratory for naturalists, some of whom may observe a particular group of nests by telescope from early dawn until sunset.

The ranch is administered by representatives from three Bay Area chapters of the National Audubon Society. It is open to the public from 10 A.M. to 4 P.M. every day but Monday from the first of March to the Fourth of July. It is free to the public, though donations are most welcome. If you can, visit the ranch during the middle of the week, for it can be crowded on weekends. During April and May the display of wildflowers is especially fine, and the rookery is noisy with the cries of young birds and the squabbles of the parents. The 1,300 acres that comprise the ranch were purchased and are maintained largely by donations from private citizens.

By all means, bring binoculars. Although there are telescopes at the Henderson Overlook, viewers are reluctant to part with them. The walk to the overlook and back makes a perfect short family jaunt. For those who wish to explore the canyon further, the *Martin Griffin Trail* provides a splendid three-mile loop. Picnickers can use the tables in

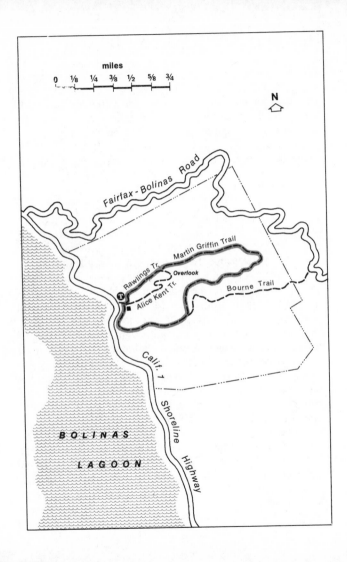

the grassy area behind the ranch museum, which houses a first-rate display of the ecology and history of the ranch. While you eat your lunch by the meandering stream, you will see both great blue herons and great egrets (formerly and less justifiably called the "common egret") sweep right over you toward their nests further up the canyon, carrying fish or perhaps a frog in their long beaks.

From San Francisco, drive north on U.S. 101 to the Mill Valley/Stinson Beach exit. Drive west for half a mile to an intersection with a traffic light. Turn left and drive for about three miles to the junction with Panoramic Highway. Either road will ultimately get you to Stinson Beach, but the signed left fork is much shorter. The highway drops down Green Gulch to Muir Beach, climbs over the coastal ridge, and drops down to the ocean side, staying high above the water until just before the town of Stinson Beach. Continue through town and along the shore of Bolinas Lagoon for three and a half miles to the ranch. It sits off the road on the right. You can recognize it by the prominent sign and the old white farmhouse. You can also get to the ranch by taking Sir Francis Drake Highway west to Olema and then turning south on Highway One. In ten miles you will come to the Bolinas junction. Keep left, coming to the ranch in about two and a half miles. Bus service is available to Audubon Canyon Ranch. Take the 62 (Bolinas) bus from the East Bay Terminal, at Fremont and Mission in San Francisco. For other stops in the city, and for exact schedules, call 332-6600.

For the shortest walk, take the *Alice Kent Trail*, which leads past the picnic area directly to the heronry overlook. This is only a half mile of easy walking, though virtually all of it is uphill. A more gradual, though slightly longer route

begins across the driveway from the caretaker's house. This
is the *Rawlings Trail*; a sign points the way. After climbing
steeply for a very short distance, you will come to an
overlook that offers a superb panorama of Bolinas Lagoon.
Notice the two alluvial fans that have developed in the
lagoon as the result of winter rains washing gravel and soil
down from nearby canyons. If left alone, the lagoon will
eventually fill up with such sediments and turn slowly into
salt marsh. If dredged to prevent this from happening, its
water flow will be altered, with unpredictable results for the
aquatic life.

You may spot an osprey from this overlook as it hovers
over the shallow waters searching for fish. This large
whitish hawk is easily recognized by black "writs" or
carpal patches on the undersides of its wings and by its habit
of diving feet-first into the water. Other hawks commonly
seen around the lagoon are the red-tailed hawk, marsh
hawk, and in winter, the red-shouldered hawk. From
October through April the lagoon plays host to thousands of
shorebirds and waterfowl, and for beginning birders it
offers a splendid introduction to most of those species of
ducks and sandpipers that commonly frequent the Bay
Area. The lagoon also boasts a reputation for rare species of
birds, accidental wanderers who will sometimes spend days
or weeks here before moving on.

After the overlook the trail climbs some more before
leveling out as it reaches the crest of the ridge. The woods
here are typical of the coastal hills, consisting largely of
Douglas fir, tanoak, California laurel, and madrone. If you
make the hike early in the season, keep an eye out for the
golden-crowned kinglet and Townsend's warbler, a small
yellow, black, and white butterfly of a bird. Also keep an

eye out for deer tracks; deer are common in the canyon and like to browse in the young Douglas firs.

Look for the sign directing you down a side trail to the overlook. As you approach it the cries of the birds get louder, until finally you can look across the canyon down to the great colony. The sight of such large birds nesting in the very tops of the redwoods is startling. You wonder how they maintain what looks to be their precarious perches, how their nests can withstand the often fierce winds that blow up this canyon.

The trees look very odd where the herons and egrets have broken off the tips, thus flattening the treetops to make their large nests of sticks. Though the number of nests varies from year to year, it is not unusual even in late June, toward the end of the season, to find as many as 140 nests housing some 50 heron and 90 egret families, and these in different stages of development from eggs to fledglings. The staggered nesting system, whereby some birds begin their households later than others, is one of nature's ways of protecting the species.

If you live near marshlands, you have probably seen both the great blue heron and the great egret many times already, but such experiences do not prepare you for the spectacle of these same enormous birds here in the redwood trees. You cannot shake the impression of incongruity and wonder that takes hold of you when you look down on the colony of nests. The extravagant nuptial plumes of the egret, the sheer size and majesty of the heron, the glorious setting of the redwoods and the distant lagoon—nature has been lavish here in this canyon, and you will find yourself remembering this scene again and again in the months and years to come.

From the Henderson Overlook you can return to your car

by taking the *Rawlings Trail* or the Alice Kent Trail, which switchbacks from the overlook down into the canyon, coming out near the picnic area behind the museum. If you wish to continue on the three-mile loop up the north side of the canyon, up over the grasslands at the rear of the canyon, and back down the other side to the ranch, return to the Rawlings Trail and turn right on the Martin Griffin Trail. Much of this walk is on old roads that are being allowed to return gradually to trails.

The whole Bolinas-Stinson Beach area seems to be sleeping in the past, and visiting the ranch is almost like stepping back to 1875, when Captain Peter Bourne built the white frame farmhouse for his bride at the mouth of this sheltered canyon facing Bolinas Lagoon. Though threatened at one time with logging and subdivision, the ranch is now safe, administered by devoted conservationists and surrounded by the Golden Gate National Recreation Area on three sides and by the watershed lands of the Marin water district on the fourth.

As you continue to walk through the woods, you may notice large deformed burls at the base of some of the laurels. According to David Cavagnaro, a photographer and naturalist living at the ranch, "There are a lot of growth buds packed that way to be resistant to fire. If that tree is killed back, or damaged by fire, a bay will stump-sprout from fire just like a redwood will. That big mass of wood is much harder to get hot or damage than if it was a spindly little trunk. The laurel will sprout; the Douglas fir will not; the old oak sometimes will, but more likely not."

At the back of the canyon the trail levels off in a thick corridor of trees. This section of the trail has the last of the fire-adapted vegetation you will see on this walk. In the spring there are the blue flowers of ceanothus, followed by clusters of white, urn-shaped flowers on the toyon, and finally, the bloom of the coffeeberry and the California hazel—all typical species of the California chaparral. Winding around the toyons are thick vines of virgin's bower (*Clematis lasiantha*) and wild honeysuckle (*Lonicera hispidula*).

There are lots of pack rats at the ranch, and if you look sharply on your left just before you get to the first redwood trees on this trail, you will see a pack-rat nest, which is shaped like an untidy igloo of sticks. Other mammals at the ranch include badger, gray fox, raccoon, bobcat, and as mentioned above, deer. Look for the scat and tracks along the trail; the animals will probably not show themselves, though you may occasionally see deer.

Near the redwoods you will find vanilla grass (*Hierochloe occidentalis*), a common associate of these forest giants, though found elsewhere as well. In the spring this long, spiky grass has showy flowers that grow in fountain shapes. The leaves, when crushed, are sweet to smell, but ''vanilla'' is stretching things a bit. Here you can see redwood stumps left from the logging of the 1860s, and on the standing trees, the scars of subsequent fires. Nearby is a tremendous stand of redwood seedlings.

You are now as high as the trail goes before it loops back down the other side of the canyon. The rookery lies down the canyon toward the west. When you look at the vegetation, it is amazing to think that this lushness has grown back within a mere century after the last major fire. When the land was first cleared of the big trees, the streams would run higher and were full of trout, but when the trees grew back they absorbed much of the runoff in their root systems. The streams grew smaller, and the trout disappeared. Steelhead still come in, but not in large numbers. Shortly, you will see Bourne's Creek, which runs by the rookery. Though it flows all year long unlike many California streams, it is much reduced in the summer.

The Martin Griffin Trail passes through the last stand of redwoods, then into thick groves of laurels. You will not find evidence of past fires on this side of the canyon, which has a much different aspect from the other, being much more open. Then, suddenly, you come out of the woods. On your left is a large field dominated by two big Douglas firs. Below are other fields, all lacking shrubs. Here the forest has not recovered so fast as on the north ridge, for this land was cleared originally for planting and grazing. The shrub formation here is not true chaparral, but north coastal scrub, which is softer leaved and not fire-adapted. Nevertheless, the two vegetation types share many species in common. Listen for the ping-pong-ball song of the wrentit, a small brown bird with a beady eye and a cocky tail that is endemic to both scrub and chaparral. The big Douglas fir you see was probably spared cutting to serve as a shade tree for cattle. It has nine trunks and is the progenitor of all the smaller firs that are slowly reclaiming this field. Here, you meet *Bourne Trail*, an old fire road that leads down to the ranch below in about three-fourths of a mile.

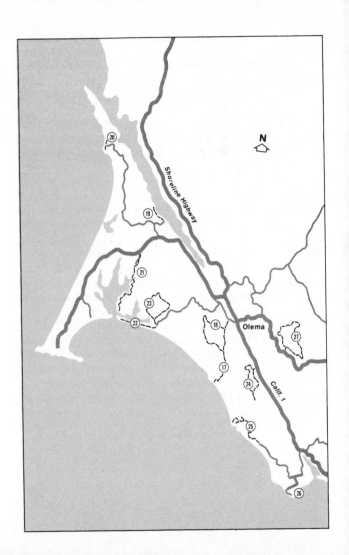

Point Reyes

FOR THE WALKER who craves wildness, spaciousness, and a measure of solitude, the Point Reyes Peninsula offers the finest hiking trails in the Bay Area. Not even the beautiful trails of Mount Tamalpais can match the sense of splendid isolation that one enjoys at Point Reyes. When walking a popular trail at Point Reyes, it is often enough to know that if you chose, you could leave the crowd and walk for miles through a virtually deserted land.

All visitors to the Point Reyes Peninsula, whether they leave their cars or not, whether they even like the place, are struck by its peculiar atmosphere. There is a haunting wildness to the peninsula, a sense not merely of solitude, but of overwhelming isolation, that cannot merely be attributed to its having remained largely undeveloped. The landscape both looks and feels different from the rest of the Bay Area, as if the peninsula were a place apart, an island hauled across the sea and fastened to the Marin coast. Indeed, geologists tell us that this is pretty much what has happened, and it seems likely that the unusual feeling of the place is grounded, though none too solidly, in this strange geographical fact.

The Point Reyes Peninsula is part of the Salinian Block, that portion of the California land mass lying west of the San Andreas Fault. Point Reyes is separated from the rest of Marin County by the Olema Valley, which traces the course of the fault along this portion of the coast. Both ends of the valley have been flooded by the ocean, forming Bolinas Lagoon in the south and Tomales Bay in the north. Movement along the fault was responsible for the San Francisco earthquake of 1906. During that quake, portions of the Point Reyes Peninsula lying adjacent to the fault in the Olema Valley jumped northward as much as twenty feet.

The land mass west of the fault began this northward movement about 40 million years ago. Since then it has continued to move at the rate of about two inches a year. Thus, Point Reyes now lies about 350 miles north of where it was first formed. Its granite bedrock, which is exposed in some places on the Inverness Ridge and in the form of Point Reyes itself, is found nowhere else in Marin County. No, it probably began as a piece of the Sierra Nevada, broken off by the fault and shipped north to the Marin coast, and it will continue to slide north, eventually becoming an island off the coast of British Columbia, and finally sinking below the sea somewhere in the Gulf of Alaska.

Perhaps this strange history accounts for the different look and feel of the Point Reyes Peninsula. Its separateness is reflected in its rocks and vegetation, which differ in certain important respects from that of the rest of Marin County. Its isolation is made physically palpable by the barrier of land and water that separates it from the land mass east of the fault. The densely forested Inverness Ridge on the south and the long arm of Tomales Bay on the north are prominent physical reminders that Point Reyes is merely a temporary visitor along this coast. One does not merely drive to Point Reyes; one drives *on* to Point Reyes. It's like entering a different world.

Point Reyes National Seashore

Most of the peninsula lies within the boundaries of the 53,000-acre Point Reyes National Seashore, which is administered by the National Park Service. Another 1,018 acres are in Tomales Bay State Park, which preserves a magnificent stretch of forested shoreline on the eastern slope of the Inverness Ridge. Together these two public parks comprise about 90 percent of the peninsula. Just below the state park is a narrow five-mile strip of private lands given over to the homes clustered about the small village of Inverness. The southern tip of the Point Reyes Peninsula, comprising the Bolinas Mesa, also lies outside the national seashore boundary. Within the park itself there are a number of private inholdings where hikers should not trespass. These lands are posted and constitute only a minute fraction of the national seashore.

The park headquarters and visitor center are located on Bear Valley Road just west of the crossroads community of Olema. Here you can obtain a trail map of the peninsula, an excellent checklist of birds, and whatever you might want in the way of field guides or other books pertaining to the area. There are natural history displays, and the rangers on duty will be happy to answer questions about the national seashore.

Overnight camping at the national seashore is limited to four backpacker camps. Spaces are limited and in great demand; if you plan a backpack trip, you should reserve your campsite well in advance by calling (415) 663-1092. For those who do not backpack, there are three campgrounds within an easy drive of the national seashore. Olema Campground Ranch, located on Highway 1 just north of Bear Valley Road, provides space for campers and trailers. Because neither is welcome at the other two campgrounds in the area, this one is usually full, and again, advance reservations may be necessary. For those who prefer old-fashioned outdoor camping, the campgrounds at

Pan Toll on Mount Tamalpais and at Samuel P. Taylor State Park are ideal. For information on Pan Toll, see the introduction to the Mount Tamalpais region. From the campground it is about a forty-five minute drive to the Point Reyes National Seashore headquarters. The campground at Samuel P. Taylor State Park is located on Sir Francis Drake Boulevard about five miles west of Olema. While you are there, you can also take the beautiful trail to the top of Barnabee Peak described in this section of the book. Motel accommodations are available in the village of Inverness, which is right next to the national seashore. Overnight camping is not permitted in Tomales Bay State Park or outside the designated sites in the national seashore.

When to Go and What to Take

Point Reyes has been much maligned as a foggy, windswept spot, but in fact, its weather is as varied as its topography, and you can expect warm sunny days any season of the year. The lighthouse at the tip of Point Reyes is apt to get the worst of the fog and wind, but on such days you can often find warmth and stillness in the deep forests of Inverness Ridge or the sheltered coves of Tomales Bay State Park on the leeward side of the peninsula. September and October are the warmest months and have the least fog and wind. Winter storms hit in December, January, and February, but the brilliant clear days in between offer some of the best hiking of the year. The rains leave the creeks rushing and full and turn the hills from brown to vivid green. May and June are beautiful months for wildflowers, and on sunny spring days the temperatures may be in the seventies. Summer is the foggiest season, but except when this moist marine layer is exceptionally heavy, the overcast may clear before noon, particularly in the areas east of Inverness Ridge.

Water safe for drinking is in short supply on the trails, so if you plan a hike of more than two hours carry your own water. Ordinary tennis shoes are acceptable for all but the longer and rougher trails. Where heavy-soled hiking boots are preferable, this has been indicated in the specific trail description. When hiking in the more open areas of the seashore, especially the beaches, protect yourself against sunburn. You might also want to wear a hat and sunglasses in these areas.

The Landscape

The Point Reyes Peninsula offers hikers three distinct types of landscape. Running parallel to the eastern border of the peninsula is the Inverness Ridge, which emerges just north of the town of Bolinas and extends north for about twenty-five miles before dropping into the sea at Tomales Point. The southern section of the ridge is covered with a mature virgin forest of Douglas fir; the middle section is dominated by bishop pine woodlands; the northern section is largely given over to grassland and scrub. The forests of the Inverness Ridge comprise the first major type of landscape at Point Reyes. Four of the hikes in this section explore these forests.

West of Inverness Ridge, a broad coastal mesa is covered with native grasslands and scrub. It is an open, windswept country reminiscent of the heaths of southern England and the moors of Scotland. This mesa faces the open Pacific on the west, where it terminates in a series of vegetated sand dunes. On the south, it culminates in the white sandstone cliffs that overlook Drake's Bay and in the bold granite headlands of Point Reyes itself. The mesa is intersected in two places by deep coastal estuaries—Drake's Estero and Limantour Estero. Three of the walks described here tour this open country west of Inverness Ridge.

The third major landscape of the Point Reyes Peninsula is its sixty-mile shoreline, which includes broad sandy beaches, dunes, sandspits, steep cliffs and headlands, and shallow salt marsh. There is a beach for all people and all seasons. Some are windy and cold much of the year; others are protected from the elements. The National Park Service maintains facilities of one sort or another at McClure's Beach, at the north and south visitor areas on Ten-mile Beach, at Drakes Beach, and at Limantour Spit. All these beaches are accessible by automobile. In addition, you can drive to Heart's Desire Cove in Tomales Bay State Park and Agate Beach, at the southwest tip of the peninsula, right next to Duxbury Reef. The beach and reef both lie outside the boundaries of the national seashore. Four of the trails in this section explore the beaches of the Point Reyes Peninsula.

The Trails

At the present time most of the trails at Point Reyes are old ranch roads left over from when the peninsula was largely given over to dairy farms. A number of these dairies are still in operation under a leasing arrangement with the Park Service, but formerly private roads are now often open to hikers. Consult the Park Service if you are in doubt about a particular route. You can walk along 100 miles of these old roads, in addition to a number of footpaths that wind up and along the Inverness Ridge. The Park Service brochure on the national seashore shows the most popular trails, but the

best hiker's map is the one published by C. E. Erickson &
Associates. It is on sale at the visitor center and at various
outlets for maps and hiking supplies throughout the Bay
Area. A topographical map is available for Point Reyes, but
it is not necessary for general use. For directions to the
various trailheads, including available bus service, consult
the specific hikes to follow.

Point Reyes National Seashore is a horseman's paradise,
although some of the trails are closed to horses on weekends
because there are so many hikers. You may bring your own
horse or rent one near the park headquarters. Most of the
trails described in this section are suitable for horses. Bike
riding is also popular at Point Reyes. Because so many of
the trails are on old ranch roads, they are often suitable for
bicycles. This is particularly true of the Bear Valley Trail
and the Coast Trail. In addition, you can bicycle on the
three main highways that explore the peninsula. The Limantour Road, which leaves the Bear Valley Road north of the
visitor center, is a stiff haul over the Inverness Ridge and a
steep drop down the other side to Limantour Estero. Easier
rides are available on Sir Francis Drake Boulevard, which
leads to Drake's Beach and Point Reyes, and on Pierce
Point Road, which ends at McClure's Beach. Bikes may be
rented just outside the park at Olema Campground Ranch.

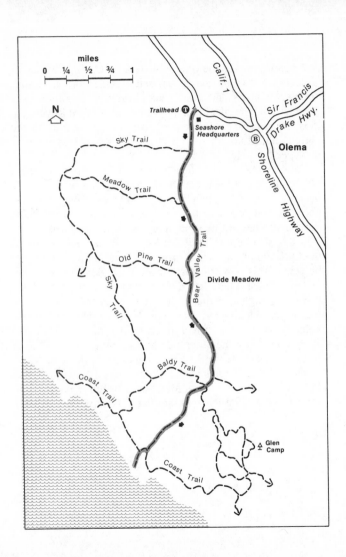

17. BEAR VALLEY

The *Bear Valley Trail* is the most popular hike at Point Reyes, combining easy walking with magnificent scenery. This old wagon road begins near the national seashore headquarters just outside Olema and meanders four and a half miles to the sea via the only low saddle on the Inverness Ridge between Bolinas Mesa and Tomales Bay State Park. The trail is virtually level from beginning to end—level enough for bikes, wheelchairs, equipment for small infants, and for anyone who can walk nine miles so long as it is not uphill. If this distance is farther than you want to walk, there is a perfect turn-around spot at Divide Meadow, about one and one-half miles from the trailhead. If you make the walk on a weekend, you will be one of hundreds of people scattered out along the trail, so for solitude, either take one of the laterals off the Bear Valley Trail or do the walk on a weekday.

From San Francisco, drive north on U.S. 101 to the Sir Francis Drake Boulevard exit to San Anselmo. In about four miles, you will come to a complicated intersection known locally as "the Hub." Keep straight ahead; Sir Francis Drake Boulevard turns left just beyond the intersection. Continue on to the town of Fairfax, from where it is about fifteen miles to Olema, on state highway 1. Turn right at Olema and in a few yards turn left on Bear Valley Road. A blue and white park sign points the way to the seashore headquarters. In about three-fourths of a mile, turn left at the park headquarters. Here you may pick up a map of the national seashore, obtain information, and purchase various field guides if you wish. You may also take the Golden Gate Transit Authority buses 62 (Bolinas) and 64 (Inverness) to Olema. To find out where to catch these buses in San

Francisco, and for exact weekday and weekend schedules, call 332-6600. Continue past the headquarters parking lot on the narrow paved road, coming in a half mile to a large dirt parking lot in an open meadow. Park here and begin your hike on the road at the gate. Here, a trail map of the entire Bear Valley area gives mileages for various routes. Depending on your time and endurance, a number of alternative hikes can be made from this point.

Between the trailhead and the coast, six lateral routes branch off the Bear Valley Trail. By combining one or more of these side trails with the main route, you can work out a number of interesting, if strenuous, loops. All provide a wilder, more solitary experience than the Bear Valley Trail itself, but entail considerable uphill walking and in most cases additional mileage. (See Section 18 for a description of one of the easier side trips.) For these trails, hiking boots are recommended, though not essential. Good walking shoes are enough for the Bear Valley Trail. Hikers unfamiliar with the trails in the area should consult the Recreational Map of Point Reyes National Seashore published by C. E. Erickson & Associates. It is available at the seashore headquarters.

You should carry a picnic lunch on this walk, regardless of whether you plan to turn around at Divide Meadow or continue all the way to the coast. Both are delightful spots for a bite of bread and cheese. Be sure to carry drinking water, for the water available from creeks and seeps along the way is not potable. For a leisurely walk to Divide Meadow and back, allow two to three hours. The round trip to the coast will take five to six hours, including time for lunch and exploring. The longer, more strenuous loops will require from six to eight hours.

You come to the first of the six side trails a short distance from the trailhead just as you are about to leave the open grasslands for the deep forest of Bear Valley. This is the *Sky Trail* up to Mt. Wittenberg, and unless you are in good shape, you might prefer another trail. The up is too up for many people. If you wish to explore the high ridge to the west, take either the *Meadow Trail* or *Old Pine Trail* farther on. Just past the Sky Trail you enter deep woods of Douglas fir, tanoak, madrone, laurel, and live oak. You will be walking in this shady forest for most of the way to the sea, the open grasslands of Divide Meadow being the only significant exception.

Bear Valley is cool and moist all year round, so dress warmly. The open grasslands by the ocean may be even chillier, thanks to summer fogs or the seemingly ever-present ocean breeze. Sunlight is sparse along this trail, and the forest is lush with trailing vines, ferns, forest shrubs, and mossy old trees. Because of the year-round moisture, vines grow rampantly along the trail—poison oak, wild honeysuckle, thimbleberry, blackberry, and salmon berry. The last three are all members of the rose family whose fruits are edible if you can beat the birds and other hikers to them.

Although the wildflowers make this hike especially fine from March through June, it is good during all seasons of the year. In the winter the woods are alive with birds, including a few species seldom or never seen here during the summer. Although spotting birds in dense forest is never easy (they always seem to duck behind a leaf just as you get your field glasses on them), your efforts will be amply rewarded along this walk. At any given time of the year, between 50 and 100 species inhabit this forest, and with a little work you can see many of them. The Bear Valley Trail is especially good because of its variety of habitats—deep forest, grasslands, streamside growth, the forest's edge. An excellent checklist of birds for Point Reyes is available at park headquarters for a modest price and is essential for any serious bird watching in the area.

The average walker, for whom the birds are but a single and delightful part of the entire scene, will find some of them so obvious and bold that they become familiar companions on the walk—the winter wren along the streamside, the raucous Stellar's jay swooping through the forest, the friendly flocks of chickadees and kinglets that loudly and busily move from tree to tree. And one bird that is always heard, but seldom seen: most any time of year, you will hear from somewhere in the vast forest a loud, high nasal note, like a little horn. If you could see the singer, you would be amazed that so big a noise could issue from so tiny a bird. This is the red-breasted nuthatch, a common resident of the conifer forest. It has the endearing habit of walking upside-down along branches in its never-ending search for insects and grubs, its insistent little horn tooting all the way.

About a half mile along the Bear Valley Trail, you will pass a second lateral trail, the *Meadow Trail*, leading off to your right. Several loops are possible using this trail. You can climb up to a junction with the Sky Trail, where you turn right to head back to the trailhead via Mount Wittenberg. Or, by turning left on the Sky Trail, you can walk south along the Inverness Ridge, rejoining the Bear Valley Trail via the *Old Pine Trail* (see Section 18) or *Baldy Trail*. You can even continue all the way to the ocean, meeting the *Coast Trail* a short distance north of where the Bear Valley Trail ends. These loops will increase your mileage substantially, and the climb up to the Sky Trail is steep.

All the way to Divide Meadow, the trail parallels a small stream that flows north back toward the trailhead. Beyond the meadow you shortly pick up another stream, this one flowing in the opposite direction of the first. This is what Divide Meadow divides: the watershed of Coast Creek, which empties into the ocean at trail's end, from that of Olema Creek, which empties into Tomales Bay. At the meadow itself, a large grassland surrounded by forest, you are standing on the lowest saddle on the Inverness Ridge. In a mile and a half, you have climbed only 200 feet. In the three miles from here to the ocean, you will descend only some 300 feet.

Divide Meadow is an ideal place for a picnic, whether you prefer to use one of the tables under the oak trees or sit in the sun out in the meadow. Those who do not wish to hike all the way to the coast can relax here—sunbathing, reading, or exploring the 110 acres of grasslands—before walking back to their cars. There are public latrines near the trail. This area was once a prime hunting spot for deer, mountain lion, game birds, and even bear.

At the south end of the meadow, the Old Pine Trail branches off to the right, climbing up to the Sky Trail. For a description of the hike up this trail and north on the Sky Trail back to the trailhead, turn to Section 18. After passing this trail, you leave the meadow to reenter the woods. Now you are walking gradually downhill, and you shortly cross Coast Creek, which will parallel the trail on your left the rest of the way. There are many excellent spots to rest by the creek.

In about a mile, you will come to the *Glen Camp Trail*, which branches uphill on the left, climbing up to grasslands and then back into forest on its way south to one of the four backpackers' camps at the national seashore. The walk from here to the Palomarin Trailhead is a spectacular route requiring an overnight stay at Glen Camp and a second car waiting for you at the other end. The route winds through forest and grasslands, explores deep canyons and broad, open headlands, passing five lakes and a waterfall, and offering some of the most sweeping views available at Point Reyes. If you wish to make this hike, you must allow at least two days and make reservations ahead of time with the Park Service for your camping spot at Glen Camp. This is the most attractive camp at Point Reyes, but the Park Service's metal barbecues and picnic tables set in concrete slabs detract from the wilderness feeling. Drinking water is available at the camp.

Just opposite the junction with the Glen Camp Trail, the Baldy Trail takes off to the right, climbing the ridge to meet the Sky Trail. You can return to the trailhead by following the Sky Trail north; this is a strenuous route recommended only for hardy walkers.

From the Glen Camp Trail, you have about a mile left before reaching the ocean. Just before getting there, the fir forest begins to thin out, giving way finally to alder groves along the stream. The view of the sea at trail's end is spectacular. You stand in lush grass on a high cliff overlooking the beach below. You can see the great sweep of the coast to the north, culminating finally in the white cliffs of Drake's Bay and the mighty granite of Point Reyes itself. Between the ocean and the forest of Inverness Ridge is a wide strip of gentle grasslands and scrub, where on a warm day, people spread out their wine and cheese and fruit, and lie only half-awake in the wild flowers, listening to the sea crashing below. This is the best of all possible worlds. Your body is just tired enough to relax completely, for your senses to drowse in the sun's warmth and the perfume of the sea.

If you wish to get down to the beach itself, the best way is to head north on the Coast Trail for perhaps a mile to the path leading down to Kelham Beach. Here you can enjoy your lunch either in the full sun on the white-sand beach or in the shade of one of the many small grottos the waves have carved in the cliffs. If you plan to walk on the beach very far, *be careful of the tides*. At high tide, the surf often beats up against the base of the cliffs, making passage impossible. Since the cliffs can be scaled in only a few places, it is absolutely essential that you keep an eye on the tides and not wander too far if you aren't sure whether the tide is coming in or going out.

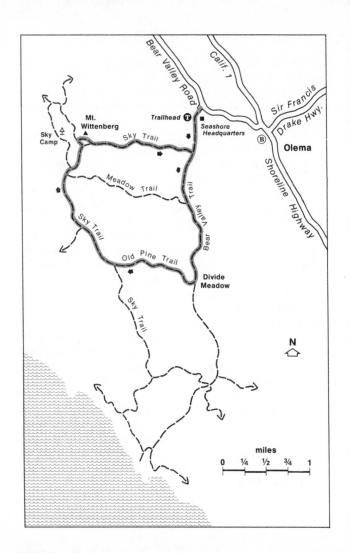

18. MOUNT WITTENBERG

From Divide Meadow on the *Bear Valley Trail*, you follow a winding foot path, the *Old Pine Trail*, up to the *Sky Trail*, which you then follow north along Inverness Ridge through Douglas fir, huckleberry, and ferns. All along the way are hidden meadows, massed with wildflowers and crossed by tempting paths. The nice thing about this walk is that you can ramble as you please and stop where you wish, enjoying the views, exploring side trails, or soaking up the sun. The walk culminates in the most sweeping view at Point Reyes, which is your reward for a short climb to the top of Mount Wittenberg.

From San Francisco, drive north on U.S. 101 to the Sir Francis Drake Boulevard exit to San Anselmo. In about four miles you will come to a complicated intersection known locally as "the Hub." Keep straight ahead; Sir Francis Drake Boulevard turns left just beyond the intersection. Continue on to the town of Fairfax, from where it is about fifteen miles to Olema, on state highway 1. Turn right at Olema and, in a few yards, turn left on Bear Valley Road. In about three-fourths of a mile, turn left at the park headquarters. Here you may pick up a map of the national seashore, obtain information, and purchase various field guides if you wish. Continue past the headquarters parking lot on the narrow paved road, coming in a half mile to a large dirt parking lot in an open meadow. Park here. You may also take the Golden Gate Transit District buses 62 (Bolinas) and 64 (Inverness) to Olema. To find out where to catch these buses in San Francisco, and for exact weekday and weekend schedules, call 332-6600.

Shortly after leaving the trailhead, which is marked by a

large map and other signs, you will pass the Sky Trail on your right just before entering the woods. This will be your route back. Only hikers who relish long steep ascents should attempt to reverse the direction given for this hike. The stretch of the Sky Trail from here to Mount Wittenberg is unnecessarily steep even now that the Park Service has placed logs across what were once straight uphill assaults on the ridge. These new switchbacks are scarcely examples of enlightened trail engineering, but they are a great improvement over the old trail and should get better as hikers continue to use them. Because of its steepness, this route should not be attempted in either direction without a good pair of heavy-soled boots. You will be grateful for the ankle support and firm grip provided by the boots on the steep downhill stretches. In normal walking shoes, you will only be increasing the possibility of turning an ankle or slipping. Also take water, for none is available along the trail.

Follow the Bear Valley Trail for a mile and a half to the south end of Divide Meadow, where you will meet the Old Pine Trail, which climbs uphill on the right for one and a half miles to the Sky Trail. The total loop is about five miles (maps and signs do not always agree at Point Reyes), and you should allow yourself from four to six hours depending on how fast you walk and how much time you like to spend resting, eating, and exploring. Except for the few steep spots in the last downward gasp from Mount Wittenberg, none of this walk is really difficult.

The Old Pine Trail leaves the Bear Valley Trail just past an old Douglas fir and climbs gently through woods dominated by alder and laurel. As you climb higher on the ridge, Douglas firs become increasingly common, finally dominating the dark forest at the top. Here the Douglas firs

have never been logged, and as a result grow close together, their foliage forming a canopy to catch the sun. The undergrowth is much thicker than below and is dominated by salal and huckleberry, two of the most handsome plants at Point Reyes. No matter what time of year you see them, they look their best. Both are members of the heath family (along with rhododendron, azalea, manzanita, madrone, and Labrador tea), the huckleberry being more common in these woods. Its stems are apt to be reddish and their evergreen leaves sharp, leathery, and pointed. In the spring the foliage is bronze tipped with red (especially where the huckleberry gets lots of sun) before turning a darker green. Only occasionally in August will you find the tasty blue-black fruit, because as soon as it is ripe the birds strip the bushes clean. Here, under the massive Douglas firs on the upper Old Pine Trail and the Sky Trail, the huckleberry bushes grow five feet tall in places.

Along the Old Pine Trail are several beautiful meadows, wide open spaces that let the Douglas firs reach an enormous girth. Green mosses cover the bark and old man's beard lichen clings to the foliage. The light comes in from all sides, so the limbs grow in all directions instead of pointing to the west as they tend to do in the denser forest. When a Douglas fir reaches out, other plants, suspended in the air so to speak, sometimes find a place to grow in the elbows formed by the branches. One of these opportunistic plants is the leather fern (*Polypodium scouleri*). You are also apt to find this tough little fern with the long "nose" or leaf tip in rock crevices on Mount Tamalpais or the Marin Headlands, but here its preferred habitat is a protected hollow on a Douglas fir.

If lucky, you might happen on a flock of red crossbills

scouring one of the Douglas firs in the meadows. These odd little finches are nowhere common in the area, but are year-round residents on Inverness Ridge, where they erratically swoop and holler in large noisy flocks. Since they are exceptionally bold, you should be able to examine them closely even without field glasses. The males are a striking brick red, and the females a dull yellow-green. Both sexes have the grotesque bill that marks the species. The upper mandible noticeably crosses over the lower, forming an ingenious tool for prying nuts out of cones.

The Old Pine Trail meets the Sky Trail at the crest of the ridge. Turn right and walk on the level in a westerly direction. Bear Valley is below you on the right. Although you cannot see the valley, you occasionally get a glimpse of the hills far to the east. On your left you can see the ridge that lies closest to the ocean. The path is pleasant underfoot, a decomposed granite that is comfortable to walk on. The forest is silent here, with only an occasional bird call breaking the stillness.

In about half a mile you will come to another meadow, this one about eighty feet wide. Here, the *Woodworth Valley Trail* sweeps down to Coast Camp and the Coast Trail. This is one of four backpackers' camps at the national seashore. Continuing on the Sky Trail, you head toward another one of these camps, Sky Camp, which is situated below Mount Wittenberg. The walk is easy along this ridge, with only occasional ups and downs.

Growing among the huckleberry in this forest is the less common but equally beautiful salal (*Gaultheria shallon*). Its stems are also reddish, but the evergreen leaves are broad and rounded, with a curly tip. Here, under the Douglas firs, salal grows three to four feet tall.

As the forest thins out, the Pacific is visible to the left. When there is no fog the water shimmers out to the horizon like a mirror tilted up to catch the afternoon light. Directly ahead and to the right you can see the bald summit of Mount Wittenberg, the highest point at the national seashore. As the trail begins to climb slightly, you will find another member of the heath family growing along the route. This is Labrador tea (*Ledum glandulosum*), whose long narrow leaves have a distinctly aromatic fragrance when pinched or broken. If you happen to forget water, they can be used as a kind of chewing gum to take the edge off your thirst. The plant can be low and spreading or waist high, as it is here. It was also valued once as providing a tea useful as a remedy for rheumatism.

About a half mile before reaching Mount Wittenberg you come to the junction with the Meadow Trail, which winds back down to Bear Valley. This is a good alternate route to either the Old Pine Trail on your way up or the Sky Trail on your way down. Its special feature is the attractive meadow about a third of the way down. From here it is a mile and a half to Bear Valley via the Meadow Trail.

From the trail that winds around Mount Wittenberg the view of Point Reyes and the sea is enormous, far more beautiful and sweeping than the better known prospect from Mount Vision, farther north on Inverness Ridge. You can see the hills undulating down to the sea and the long line of surf breaking on the beaches. Far to the west beyond Drake's Bay, Point Reyes rises steeply from the water. To the south, near the horizon, lie the Farallones. At your feet, the wildflowers grow so profusely in the spring that it is almost impossible not to step on them if you cut through the grass. You can climb to the very top of Mount Wittenberg or simply make a big circle around the peak on the road below. Directly below the road to the west is Sky Camp, which will give you a good idea of what the overnight campsites at Point Reyes are like. Sky Camp is certainly one of the better camps because of the incredible view and good drinking water. Reservations are required for all the backpackers' camps, and it is a good idea to make them well ahead of time.

The Sky Trail drops steeply from Mount Wittenberg to the Bear Valley Trailhead. Here is where good boots will come in handy. The trail alternates between deep woods and open grasslands. The ridge is drier here than along the Old Pine Trail, and on a hot day the long stretches of open country can be uncomfortable. You might want to take a hat. The total mileage of this loop adds up a little differently depending on whose map you use, but five miles seems close enough. You can spend four hours on the upper trails and never feel pressed for time because the last mile and a half is a fast downhill walk. You can stop to look for the shy birds that rustle in the bushes along the way or take side trails to see special views. There is a particular satisfaction in finding your own private field crowded with wildflowers, from the gaudy iris to the fragile shooting star or the unexpected columbine. Allow a little extra time in the spring for exploring these verdant sky meadows. This loop offers you three large separate meadows and three smaller ones from which to choose your own special garden.

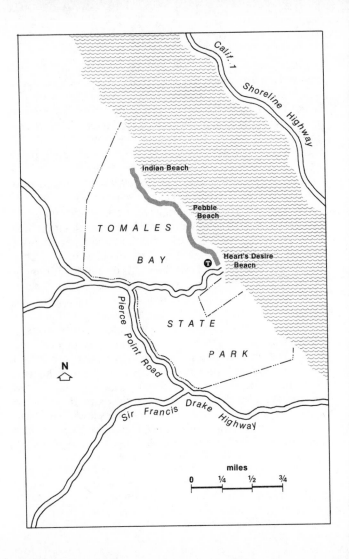

19. TOMALES BAY STATE PARK

Nowhere in Northern California is the course of the San Andreas Fault so clearly marked as it is in west Marin County. Running briefly out to sea north of San Francisco, the fault strikes land again at Bolinas Lagoon. From there it proceeds north up the Olema Valley, which is a seismic trough created by uplift along a fault line, rather than a true valley, which is carved by a river. The fault runs out to sea again just north of the town of Olema. Here, Tomales Bay, a long finger of ocean extending southward, has submerged the Olema Valley for some twelve miles. The bay dramatically shows how the Point Reyes Peninsula on the west is separated from the rest of Marin County by the fault. Here you are on the border of two of the major plates of the earth's crust. To the east lies the North American plate, to the west, the Pacific Plate. Movement along the fracture separating the two accounts for the frequent earthquakes along the San Andreas Fault.

Tomales Bay State Park is situated along the bay a few miles north of the town of Inverness. Its charming coves, which are backed by a dense forest of bishop pines, look across the calm waters to the grassy hills of west Marin. On the days when gray mists settle thickly over gray hills and gray water, the area can seem curiously depressing, or at least moody, but when the sun shines, the sandy coves of Tomales Bay are among the brightest, most picturesque spots in the Bay Area. The beaches here lack the drama of the Pacific shore because they are on a deep inlet, which so reminded early Scottish settlers in the area of the firths of their homeland that they named their local village Inverness. But if the area lacks the power of the open sea, its waters are calm enough and warm enough that children can safely splash and swim in the shallow coves. While Heart's Desire Beach is accessible by a road through the state park, the other coves require a walk through the magnificent forest of Bishop pines. Naturally, Heart's Desire Beach is the most crowded of the coves, so for a quieter scene, head for Indian Cove.

From San Francisco, drive north on U.S. 101 to the Sir Francis Drake Boulevard exit. Head west to San Anselmo, arriving in four miles at the "Hub," a complicated intersection where Sir Francis Drake Boulevard makes a broad left turn. Drive two miles to the town of Fairfax and another fifteen miles to Olema. Turn right on Highway 1. In two miles Sir Francis Drake Boulevard turns left to skirt the mudflats on the south end of Tomales Bay. Then it swings north up the west shore of the bay to Inverness. Drive past Inverness. The road climbs over a low saddle in the Inverness Ridge to the junction with Pierce Point Road. Take the right fork and drive for a mile or so to the entrance to Tomales Bay State Park.

All along the edge of Tomales Bay you will see fishermen. In season, they can expect both silver salmon and steelhead. The mudflats at the south end of the bay are excellent for shorebirds from early fall through late spring. Each winter for the past several years, a bald eagle has visited this section of the bay.

The town of Inverness is marked by a post office, a grocery, a coffee house, a restaurant, and the last available gas station. Both the village and the bay are protected from the winds coming off the Pacific by the Inverness Ridge, which rises abruptly to the west. The lucky people who live on the crest of the ridge not only have the Point Reyes

National Seashore at their back doors, but can often see the Pacific from one window and Tomales Bay from another.

As you drive through the state park down to Heart's Desire Beach, the bishop pine forest closes around you. With their picturesque shapes, dense, ink-green foliage, and the lush understory beneath them, the bishop pines are among the most beautiful trees along the coast. When you examine the needles you will find that they grow in clusters of two, which is a sure way to distinguish them from the very similar Monterey pine, whose needles are grouped in threes. Both pines have small closed cones that grow very close to the branches. These cones require intense heat, as in a forest fire, before they will open to release their seeds. For this reason both the bishop and Monterey pines are known as "fire pines." The knobcone pine of the hot California interior ranges is a close relative. Like the Monterey pine, the bishop is considered a relict species that has passed its finest hour. Bishop pines are slow to spread, but they have colonized open grasslands at various spots around Point Reyes. Farther north along the coast these pines form extensive forests that run to the ocean's edge.

An abundance of Indian relics have been uncovered at Tomales Bay State Park, which is no wonder, since it is one of the most protected, congenial spots on the Point Reyes Peninsula. Here, life must have been easy, with plenty of fish and waterfowl, tule reeds for boats and baskets, the shelter of the bay, and an abundance of berries in the forest. This is not to mention the numerous mounds of clam shells scattered about the area, which would indicate that this shellfish may have well been the mainstay of their diet, as it was for many California Indian tribes.

Heart's Desire Beach is covered with crushed clam and

oyster shells. It is not wide, but very pleasant. If you wish to combine a short walk through the forest with your day at the beach, however, take the beautiful half-mile trail to Indian Beach. The slim, white-barked trees along the way are red alders, and perhaps the most magnificent laurel in the Bay Area is located near the midpoint of this walk.

Indian Beach is a larger version of Heart's Desire Beach. The water is calm enough to paddle from one beach to the other if you have a small, lightweight boat. This is a fine place for kayaks, canoes, and small sailboats. Indian Beach is longer than Heart's Desire, but it is also very narrow. It is fringed with pickleweed (*Salicornia virginica*), a succulent, fleshy plant that grows only in salt marshes, thriving in water containing as much as 6.5 percent salts. It is a halophyte, that is, a plant able to selectively maintain its salt level by osmosis.

From the number of animal tracks on the beach, you can imagine the activities that must go on here at night after the last visitors have left. Raccoon prints are most common, along with the hoof prints of deer, but with some patience you will be able to pick out the prints of other animals as well. The tiny mice that live in intricate passages in the pickleweed are so light-footed that only the tiniest signs of disturbance indicate their runways.

The outlook, over toward the settlement at Marshall on the opposite side of Tomales Bay, with the rather barren hills behind, is a complete contrast to the lush vegetation of Tomales Bay State Park. In the waters just offshore you can see a number of birds, especially during the winter or when the anchovies are running up the bay. At such a time, the water may be completely spangled with these tiny fish, as they dash frantically before larger predatory fish. Anchovies are a favorite diet item for virtually every fish-eating fish, fowl, or mammal in and over the sea. Loons, grebes, diving ducks such as the magnificent black and white common goldeneye, pelicans, gulls, porpoises, and virtually all larger fish relish the hapless anchovy. Fortunately, even with commercial fishing, there still seem to be enough to go around. Given the crucial role the anchovy plays in the diets of most sea predators, it behooves mankind to take whatever steps are necessary to guarantee their continued abundance.

As you walk back to your car, you may notice an excited flock of tiny gray birds moving haphazardly through the bishop pines, crying "ti-di, ti-di" incessantly, and hanging upside down from the branches of the trees. These are pygmy nuthatches, bold little mites who especially favor the coastal pine forests. Though many other species of birds share the pines with the nuthatch, this busybody of the forest is an appropriate emblem to remind you of your visit to Tomales Bay State Park.

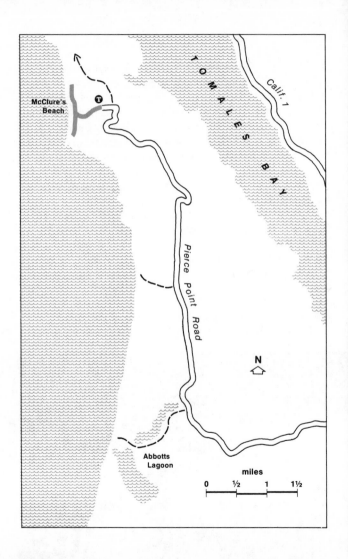

20. McClure's Beach

For people who like their beaches dramatic, with huge rocks and pounding surf, the most beautiful in Marin must be McClure's Beach on the northwestern shore of the Point Reyes Peninsula. Of all the places described in this book, McClure's is the farthest from San Francisco, an all-day excursion for most residents of the Bay Area. There are several routes to Point Reyes National Seashore, but from San Francisco, the fastest is probably via Sir Francis Drake Boulevard. For an excellent alternate route, however, drive north on U.S. 101 through San Rafael to the Lucas Valley Road exit. Turn left under the freeway and head west past a suburban housing tract before finally plunging into the beautiful countryside. Follow this meandering road for ten miles, meeting a second road just south of Nicasio. Turn right, driving through this charming, out-of-the-way village, and around the northern shore of Nicasio Reservoir until you meet a larger highway, which comes in from Petaluma. Turn left, continuing along the lake and down a narrow canyon to yet another road. Turn right and drive for a couple of miles to Highway 1 just above the town of Point Reyes Station, the largest settlement in the area. Turn left and drive through the town. After crossing a bridge over Lagunitas Creek, turn right on Sir Francis Drake Boulevard, which winds along the shore of Tomales Bay to the village of Inverness. After leaving the town, the road winds along the bay for a ways before turning inland, winding over a saddle in Inverness Ridge to the junction with Pierce Point Road. Take the right fork and drive for ten miles to the road's end and McClure's Beach.

The Pierce Point Road is a pleasure to drive, though it

can seem to go on forever if you are anxious to get to the beach. After it leaves Sir Francis Drake Boulevard skirting the bishop pine forest that marks the boundary of Tomales Bay State Park, it provides a magnificent view of the central portion of the Point Reyes Peninsula. The land falls off abruptly to your left, the pines giving way to rolling grasslands punctuated by isolated groves of pines and cypress and small stock ponds that gleam in their hollows like jewels. You see ranch buildings in the distance and the large blue expanse of Abbot's Lagoon, a former estuary that was eventually shut off from the ocean by the advancing sandspit at its mouth.

When you come to the lagoon you can park by the side of the road, pass through the fence on the south side of the lagoon and follow faint trails through the hills to the sea. In the winter and early spring this area is thick with birds. Look for widgeon and the beautiful cinnamon teal among them on the lagoon. Among the other ducks that frequent this large freshwater pond are mallard, canvasback, ruddy duck, and pintail. Marsh hawks, red-tailed hawks, and kestrels patrol the area in impressive numbers. The beach, which lies at the far end, is a beautiful strand for a warm, calm day, but can be bitterly cold during wind or fog.

But to get to McClure's Beach, pass up Abbot's Lagoon and, a short way down the road, the stile marking the trail to Kehoe Beach. The road climbs abruptly to the crest of the narrow peninsula, from which you can see Tomales Bay on the east and the Pacific on the west. Below, to your left you get a glimpse of the parking lot at the head of the short trail to McClure's Beach, and to your right, a sprawling old white frame house and dairy, which once belonged to Margaret McClure. She was one of the first people to open a beach at Point Reyes to the public, donating her beach, along with an adjacent fifty-two acres, to the county in 1942 for use as a park. It is now part of the Point Reyes National Seashore.

Follow the sandy foot trail that leads beside the stream for

a half mile down to one of the most dramatic beaches in the Bay Area. The south end of the beach has towering, striated rocks or stacks, which are thrust straight up from the sea. These granite monuments were carved by the surf from the steep cliffs that rise steeply from the beach, forming a crescent that provides protection enough on some days to allow sunbathing even in winter. You can climb through a narrow passageway between the rocks and come out on a smaller, even more dramatic beach. The sand is so clean that the tides must come in high along here. The force of the waves against the stubborn rocks throws huge plumes of spray high over the stacks. On the rocks at low tide you can examine the remarkably hardy sea palms (*Postelsia palmaeformis*) an intertidal brown alga up to two feet tall, which forms miniature forests despite the most unmerciful pounding by the surf.

Here at McClure's Beach are some of the few tide pools in Marin County, other than those of Duxbury Reef, which are easily accessible. Because of the seastacks, large and small, this is prime habitat for mussels, which are so prolific on the rocks that from a distance they resemble some kind of purple moss. (Gathering mussels, either for fishing or eating, is strictly prohibited at the national seashore.) Mussels prefer to remain submerged much of the time, so they tend to grow on the lower part of the rocks, the upper border of the colony roughly marking mean sea level. They are so much creatures of the surf that away from it they grow much smaller; the best specimens thrive where the waves crash the hardest. The dense colonies provide shelter for other creatures such as sponges, snails, worms, and crabs. Except at the lowest tides, it is usually impossible to examine closely these odd collections of life. During the summer mussels are extremely dangerous to eat because they concentrate the deadly *gonyaulax*. So even where you can legally gather them, do not do so without first consulting the State Department of Fish and Game, or other experts, as to the safety of eating them.

Barnacles generally live on the higher, more exposed portions of the rocks, clustered where they can catch just enough spray. You will see a few of the large goose barnacles, their odd stems giving them a special, long-necked advantage in big breakers. The giant green anemone is the most dramatic inhabitant of these tidepools. If you touch its emerald-green tentacles, it will suddenly withdraw into a dull olive doughnut, which will squirt a little sea water at you should you happen to step on it.

At the south end of this hidden cove at McClure's Beach is a huge rounded rock just offshore, where you are likely to see brown pelicans, cormorants, and common murres. The big brown pelicans will sun themselves on this rock and are often present in large numbers. The juvenile birds are told from the adults by their dark heads and white breasts. In the adults this coloring is just reversed. Every now and again one of these magnificent birds will take off from the rock, spreading its huge wings for a solitary flight up the shore.

If you look offshore, you may notice small black objects bobbing up and down in the rolling swells, riding high on a crest, then disappearing into a trough between the waves. These are surf scoters, a sea duck common in the Bay Area. It is found in protected bays as well as the open ocean. You can recognize it by the all-black body, the black and white head, and the bright, oddly shaped orange and white bill. Two other scoters are seen less frequently at Point Reyes: the white-winged scoter is identified by its white wing patch and teardrop-shaped eye spot; and the black scoter has a bright orange knob on its bill and is the only all black duck in North America. It is also the least common of the three in this area.

21. DRAKE'S ESTERO

Although the rolling grasslands west of Inverness Ridge are officially part of the Point Reyes National Seashore, they are still used by their former owners, under leases from the Park Service, as rangelands for both beef and dairy cattle. Public access is limited to a few old ranch roads that serve as trails. The best of these is the *Drake's Estero Trail*, which offers superb views and abundant wildlife.

If you walk all the way to where the estero opens out to the sea, you will have covered about four and a half miles, making the complete trip an all-day project. A loop trip is possible, but most people will prefer simply to return the way they came. You will need good walking shoes or boots (tennis shoes may not be adequate), a lunch, and a canteen of water. If there is any trail that merits taking a pair of field glasses, this is it. You will want them for birds, deer, even seals and giant bat rays.

From San Francisco, drive north on U.S. 101 for about ten and a half miles to the Sir Francis Drake Boulevard exit to San Anselmo. Drive through Kentfield and Ross to "the Hub," where you keep straight ahead through the intersection. The road then quickly swings left. Drive another fifteen miles to Olema. Turn right on Highway 1 and drive two miles, where Sir Francis Drake Boulevard turns left just before a bridge. Continuing up the west shore of Tomales Bay, the road takes you through the town of Inverness, where gasoline and supplies are available. Beyond Inverness the road climbs over a low saddle in Inverness Ridge to the junction with Pierce Point Road, which leads to Tomales Bay State Park and McClure's Beach. Keep left at the junction, winding down through a stream bottom thick with alders and shrubs. Continue past the Mount Vision Road on

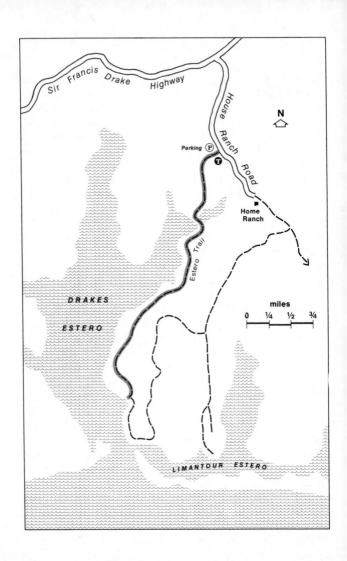

your left and begin looking for a blue-and-white park sign reading "Drake's Estero Trail." Turn left at the sign on a narrow dirt road and follow it to the parking lot at the trailhead.

The best time to make this hike is probably in the month of March, when the spring wildflowers have begun to bloom and the wintering birds on the estero (the Spanish word for estuary) have not yet left for their northern breeding grounds. Even the clearest winter days can be cold and blustery out on these open hills. In the summer the birds and wildflowers are largely gone, though the excellent views remain. Take sunglasses and a hat if you make this walk on a sunny day because there is precious little shade available. During the winter, dress in several layers of clothing that you can put on and take off as the weather indicates. It can be warm and still in the morning, only to turn fiercely windy and cold in the late afternoon.

From the parking lot, pass through the stile and walk up the dirt road through the mixed herd of hereford and black angus cattle that seem to hang around this trailhead. Although these cows are not the brave bulls of Spain, there may be a black angus bull or two in the herd. You'll know them when you see them. Though they pose little threat to the hiker, it's best to give them a wider berth than you would the rest of the herd, which is composed of docile cows. These more easily intimidated beasts usually will stop their chewing and stare at you as you pass, though occasionally one or two will turn and gallop off for a short distance. You will encounter cattle at several points along this trail; they are nothing to worry about. Watching the young calves, in fact, as they gambol about the field—and they *do* gambol—is delightful.

The road climbs easily to the crest of the low, grassy hills and swings left to make a long easy descent to the young pines, originally planted as a tree farm, at the head of Home Bay. Along the way you will pass a huge old cypress below the trail. The only tree of any size along this entire walk, it often houses songbirds of various kinds and for a birdwatcher is probably worth a few minutes' pause. Right from the start the views are sweeping. You can see Home Bay itself and the surrounding hills. Look for deer, either the black-tail deer native to the area, or the imported axis deer, which is pure white and boasts a larger set of antlers than the black-tail. Wildflowers are generally scarce along this trail, thanks to grazing, but in the spring Douglas iris and bush lupine make a fine display. It is useful to compare the relative scarcity of flowers on this walk with the abundance of bloom to be found on the hills above Limantour Estero not far away. The difference is cattle.

After passing the pines the road swings left across a weir dividing Home Bay on your right from a large pond on your left. This pond once served a duck club, and during the winter it still attracts many species of waterfowl. You may also see loons and grebes on the pond, but you are more likely to find them out on the open bay. The mudflats on your right as you cross the weir are good places to view shorebirds—willet, kildeer, dunlin, least and western sandpipers, lesser yellowlegs, and many others. Great blue herons are invariably either standing erect in the shallow water or skulking about the mudflats in slow deliberate steps, their baleful eyes searching for fish. Sometimes flocks of snowy egrets will perch in low trees along the estero.

To best see the birds of the estero, follow the road, which

climbs the cliff overlooking the water. Once on top you have an excellent view of the mudflats and water below. A rest here will turn up many species of birds—shorebirds, herons and egrets, ducks, grebes, and loons. Virtually any bird that is found in saltwater habitats around the Bay Area can be identified in this estero during the winter. If you are lucky, you might also see in the clear, shallow waters below, one of the most ghostly sights in nature—a giant bat ray "flying" just beneath the surface, its enormous triangular wings flapping in slow, rhythmical strokes. This creature is enormous and seems like a monster from an alien world, though it is really quite harmless, unlike its close relatives the stingray and electric ray. A denizen of shallow bays and estuaries such as this, it feeds on crabs and shellfish, which it stirs from the sandy bottom with each beat of its vast wings.

You may also see either harbor seals or California sea lions in the estero. Seals and sea lions belong to two different families of the same order—*Pinnipeda*—and are distinguished by several major, if not prominent, anatomical differences. Sea lions have tiny external ears, powerful front flippers, large back flippers that can be brought together underneath them for locomotion on land, and well-developed nails only on the three middle digits of the hind flippers. Seals have no external ears, smaller front flippers, back flippers that cannot be used for movement on land, and well-developed nails on all five digits of their rear flippers. There are four species of sea lions and two of seals native to the California coast, and of these only the harbor seal and the California sea lion regularly enter bays and estuaries. You can most easily distinguish the two by their color: the harbor seal tends to be lighter, though not necessarily. The California sea lion is the performing "seal" of the circus. If you find a seal staring at you as you walk along the water, even coming out to get a better look, chances are it is a harbor seal, which is well known for its curiosity. Also, you are not likely to see a sea lion in the summer months, when they have gone south to breed. Harbor seals breed in the Bay Area, as well as other places along the California coast.

The trail continues along the cliff for some ways before turning inland and dropping down to a small pond, where you may scare up a few pintails or canvasbacks. When it climbs back on top of the hills again, the estero will be much farther away to the west. You will drop down to a second, larger pond, with even greater numbers of ducks, and climb once again to the hilltops. As you move along the views of the estero and surrounding landscape become increasingly panoramic. You can see Point Reyes off to the south, the ocean in the west, and Inverness Ridge to the northeast. The water of the estero is as blue as the sky and in the summer provides a stunning contrast to the golden hills. Drake's Estero consists of many narrow fingers that probe deeply into the coastal hills. As you continue toward the coast these several ''bays'' come into view. The estero is much larger than it first seemed to be. In winter look for armadas of white pelicans cruising in the middle of the estero. In flight, you will know them because they look like the biggest white bird you've ever seen—at least the biggest with black borders on their wings. These majestic relatives of the coastal brown pelican nest inland on such desert lakes as Pyramid Lake in Nevada and the Great Salt Lake in Utah. They like to spend their winters on the coast.

The trail keeps well above the bay, winding through grassland and coastal scrub. It is a fragrant walk on a warm spring day, for these hills are covered in certain places with bush lupine. As you walk don't hesitate to make short forays into the hills or down toward the water. In open country like this it is impossible to get lost. If you feel like just rambling cross country, you can do it here. If you need to get your bearings, just climb to the top of a hill.

You will know the end of the trail is near when you see a couple of small ponds before you, with the estero and ocean behind them. The trail leads down into the draw containing these ponds, and on a windy day you can usually find a protected spot somewhere around here to eat lunch. If you are a birdwatcher, approach these ponds with caution, for they often host several species of ducks, including green-winged teal, which normally wouldn't spend much time—if any—on the adjacent salt water.

At low tide you can easily make your way out along the estero at the base of the cliffs on your left. (In high tide you can cut directly uphill from the ponds, and wander over the grasslands to the edge of Limantour Estero to the east or to the cliffs facing the ocean to the south.) Straight ahead, you can see the narrow channel to the sea between Drake's Beach on your right and Limantour Spit on your left. As you round the point of land, all of Drake's Bay opens before you. Far to the southeast lies the San Francisco Peninsula. In the same direction, though closer, you can see the wooded Inverness Ridge rising above the sea, and the long cliff-lined shore sweeping in a great arc toward where you stand. Across the estero rise the chalk-colored cliffs of Drake's Beach, which swings south on an even tighter curve to culminate in the granite headlands of Chimney Rock. Directly to the left you can see the long arm of Limantour Estero walled up behind the dunes, its only outlet to the sea being the one before you. During very low tides, it is possible to continue along the base of the cliffs, exploring the tidepools, until you come to a ranch road, which leads straight up to the hilltops. From here you can cut across the rolling grasslands back in the general direction of the ponds.

On these cliffs overlooking Drake's Bay, you are standing in a place of historical controversy. The question that both sides continue to debate with vigor is whether, in June of 1579, Sir Francis Drake, the legendary privateer in the service of Queen Elizabeth I, sailed into Drake's Bay or San Francisco Bay. If the latter, then he was the first European to do so; but if he sailed instead into Drake's Bay, then San Francisco Bay went undiscovered for another two centuries. We know he called his anchorage "Nova Albion" (New

England) "in respect of the white banks and cliffs, which lie toward the sea," and which must have reminded him of the chalk cliffs of Dover. From where you stand you can see such white cliffs as Drake described. We also know that he built a fortification, though no traces of it have been found either here or on San Francisco Bay. Finally, we know he left a brass plate commemorating his visit tacked to a post. What is almost surely this plate, judging from expert analysis of the age of the metal and other details, now lies in the Bancroft Library at the University of California at Berkeley. It was discovered in 1936 near San Quentin Prison, which is situated on the shore of San Francisco Bay, on the other side of Marin County from Drake's Estero. At first this seemed to settle once and for all that Drake had indeed discovered San Francisco Bay. But shortly after the brass plate was uncovered, a man turned up who claimed to have picked up the plate near Muddy Hollow, which is only a mile from Drake's Bay. He said he didn't know what it was at the time but kept it anyway, throwing it away later at San Quentin. If he is right, then Drake's Bay was indeed the anchorage of the *Golden Hinde*, but we will probably not know for sure until, and if, Drake's lost journals sometime show up. He presented them to Queen Elizabeth after the completion of his round-the-world voyage. If she and her successors took care of them, the journals may yet be found in the depths of some English archives, but until then, the controversy over which bay Drake discovered is likely to continue unabated.

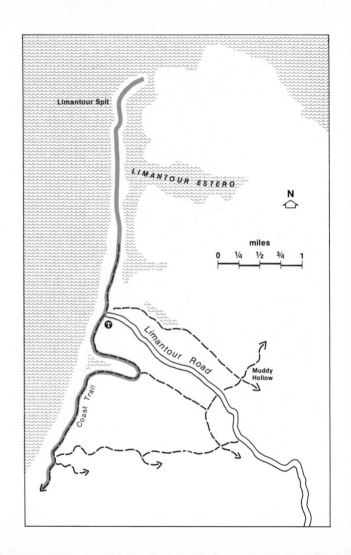

22. LIMANTOUR SPIT

Once a rare, isolated beach known only to birdwatchers, who had to get permission to enter the area, Limantour Spit is now among the most popular beaches in Marin County, thanks largely to a broad, ill-advised highway that the National Park Service constructed over Inverness Ridge between Bear Valley and the coast. What was once a lonely, nearly inaccessible strand is now crowded every warm weekend with people. Yet it is still less crowded than Stinson Beach, if only because it is farther from the more populous sections of Marin County. It is also more extensive than Stinson Beach, which it resembles in a way, so that it's easier to get away from the beach blankets and footballs, provided you are willing to walk a ways. But for real solitude, come here on a weekday or during the winter, when the weather can be fit for a walk even if it is too brisk for lying on the sand.

From San Francisco, drive north to the Sir Francis Drake Boulevard exit to San Anselmo. Drive through Kentfield and Ross to "the Hub," where Sir Francis Drake Boulevard makes a broad left turn. Drive another fifteen miles to Olema. Turn right on Highway 1 and shortly thereafter turn left on Bear Valley Road. Continue past the seashore headquarters. Just past the point where the road leaves the woods and makes a noticeable turn toward the west, turn left on the road leading to Limantour Estero. Drive far enough and you'll end up in the parking lot.

An additional reason for visiting Limantour Spit during the winter is that the estuary lying directly behind this long finger of dunes is one of the major wintering grounds for waterfowl and shorebirds along the northern California coast. This is one of the few places in the Bay Area where eel grass is still plentiful enough to support a large population of black brant, the West's magnificent sea goose. On a typical winter day some fifteen species of waterfowl and at least an equal number of shorebird species can be found in the estuary and ocean at Limantour. Rarities are seen here throughout the year.

The dunes of Limantour tell stories. It was here that the local Indians came to hunt for waterfowl and clams. Almost 200 diggings have been mapped out, carefully sectioned, and recorded. Many are still being explored. Apparently the Indians used Limantour much as we do—living in the protected inland hills and valleys and visiting the shore on special occasions such as feasts. Fine black lines in the shaved-off sands of the archeological sites indicate a floor of crushed charcoal, where the Indians cooked their meals.

Limantour Beach has no lifeguards and a more dangerous surf than Stinson Beach, but it is still possible to wade out hip deep and ride the waves back. But remember, the water along this coast is never warm. Most walkers and lovers of wildness will be happy to trade the amenities of Stinson Beach for the emptiness of Limantour and its enormous sweep of beach. Except on weekends, there is a wildness here that is not interrupted by any sound but that of the sea itself. When the wind picks up, as it is apt to do about three or four in the afternoon, move back into the dunes, where you can find your own private protected spot amid the white sand and tall grass.

In the fresh dune sands you will see the trails of small insects and mice that live in the grass. Overhead, marsh hawks and red-tailed hawks patrol the shore. In the estero egrets and herons stab fish in the shallow water, while dabbling ducks turn tails up to probe in the mud. A loon may suddenly surface on the water like a little submarine, idly swimming for a bit before diving for another bite to eat. Everywhere the estero is animated with the ceaseless activities of birds, the squawks and squabbles, the flocks of shorebirds rising in alarm if you press too near, the noisy honking of the geese. Such aggregations of birds are the only mass displays of wildlife available in most of the United States. One derives energy from the sheer number of birds and can sense, in small degree, what the impact of the vast herds of buffalo that once roamed the plains must have been, what that of the African herds still is. Life in such force and numbers is intoxicating.

Limantour is the best walking beach in the Bay Area. From the parking lot you can walk west along the spit for some two miles before the land gives out just across from the white cliffs of Drake's Bay. Finally, you come to the narrow channel to the sea that feeds both Limantour Estero and nearby Drake's Estero. At low tide the mudflats here are excellent for viewing shorebirds.

If you head east down the beach from the parking lot, you can walk another two miles before the surf meets the cliffs at high tide. At low tide you can venture even farther. Just above the beach, the *Coast Trail* leads to Coast Camp, one of four backpackers' camps at the national seashore, and beyond that to the *Bear Valley Trail* and eventually to the *Palomarin Trailhead* at the southern tip of the park. You may also take a walk inland to Muddy Hollow or follow the loop trip described in the following section.

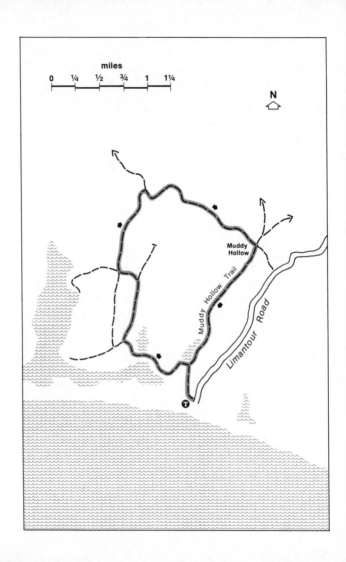

23. MUDDY HOLLOW LOOP

This hike is not for everyone. It is about six miles long, there is very little shade along the way, and the trail is not always easy to find. You have to walk through boggy spots where your boots are sure to get wet, watch out for poison oak, and jump a stream that is just wide enough to make you wonder. But there are ample compensations for those willing to pay the modest price: abundant wildflowers, perhaps the richest birding in the Bay Area, and a measure of solitude not easily found within a hundred miles of San Francisco. As a bonus, the views are marvelous—fog creeping in probing fingers or broad drifts, the sweeping panorama of forest and grasslands and broad blue sea, the shimmer of secluded ponds and lagoons nestled in the hills.

Be sure to take water, for the Park Service warns that the streams in this area are unsafe. You should also take a lunch; this is an all-day hike, and you will want something to eat long before you are through. Hiking boots are strongly recommended because of the cross-country stretches and boggy places. Yet all considered, this is not a difficult hike, the route is mostly level and the distance is only moderate. But whatever you do, wear a hat, on windy days to keep your head warm and on sunny days to keep it protected. You should also consider taking sunglasses and perhaps a good tanning lotion. Properly equipped and with a whole day ahead, you should have a splendid adventure.

From San Francisco, drive north on U.S. 101 to the Sir Francis Drake Boulevard exit to San Anselmo. In about four miles you will come to a complicated intersection known locally as "the Hub"; swing left with Sir Francis Drake Boulevard and follow it fifteen miles to Olema. Turn right on Highway 1, and then left on the road leading to the Point Reyes National Seashore headquarters. Here you may pick up a map of the seashore, along with various field guides and brochures. On this hike, a good wildflower guide and bird guide to the area are musts for the amateur naturalist. Both are available at the visitor center. Continue past the headquarters on the same road for about a mile and a half to the junction with the Limantour Estero Road, which takes off on the left. A sign will direct you. This road winds up over Inverness Ridge and down the other side, behaving much like a roller coaster until it finally ends at the parking lot at Limantour Estero. Park as close as you can get to the public latrines. Take the path from the parking lot down past the latrines, where you turn right on an old road. The path is marked with a blue park sign showing a hiker, the road with a sign reading "Limantour Trailhead." A second sign reads "Bayview, 3.7 miles."

You begin the hike at the Limantour parking lot, which is packed with cars each sunny weekend. The beach along Limantour Spit is justifiably one of the most popular at the Point Reyes National Seashore. Yet a few feet beyond, you leave people for birds and pavement for wildflowers. Occasionally you will meet a solitary hiker working his way over the downs, but on this hike such rare encounters are brief, welcome interludes to the solitude of the day. You smile with the shared joy of knowing a special place far from the madding crowd.

If you are the sort who likes to roam freely through a landscape, reveling in brightness and wildness and open vistas, this hike is for you. If you prefer to walk slowly, examining each new wildflower that decks your path, identifying each new bird that claims the air, this hike is also for you. It takes time; you will be tired; your feet will demand a rest at the end of the day; but your spirit will be refreshed and your senses rewarded.

In late winter and early spring the coastal hills are ablaze with wildflowers, and of these the most glorious is the Douglas iris (*Iris douglasiana*), a flower so large and showy that you can hardly believe it has not escaped from a garden. Ranging in color from white, through pale blues and lavenders, to magenta and deep purple, this native iris blooms abundantly near the coast, usually in dense clumps of a dozen blossoms or more. You will notice them on this hike immediately as you step from your car—if you come at the right time—for they bloom in profusion all around the parking lot. You will be walking among them for most of the day.

The best time to take this hike is between February and May. What you are trying to do in scheduling this walk is to hit that perfect time when the thousands of shorebirds and waterfowl that winter in the estero have not yet left for their northern nesting grounds, and when the spring wildflowers that turn these grassy coastal hills into a garden have begun to bloom. Then you have the best of both worlds—land and sea alike contributing to your pleasure. Summer is perhaps the least spectacular season to make this hike, but since much of the appeal of this country lies in its changing moods, as well as its specific attractions, even summer can be charming, when the coastal fog sweeping over the downs makes this land resemble nothing so much as the moors of Scotland.

As you walk along the dirt road that parallels Limantour Estero, you may be faced with a surfeit of attractions, to the point where you do not know what to look at first—several species of ducks swimming in the deeper waters of the lagoon—pintail, canvasback, shoveler, common widgeon, mallard, gadwall, scoters; shorebirds on the mudflats—willets, sanderlings, dowitchers, dunlins, lesser yellowlegs; great blue herons and great egrets probing the tidal sloughs, loons and grebes cruising the channels. Limantour Estero is one of the last pristine estuaries on the California coast, and each winter it hosts thousands of birds, which find here the measure of food and solitude that has so commonly been deprived them elsewhere. One special attraction of the estuary is the large flock of brant geese that come here each winter to feed on the eel grass. Many years ago brant also wintered on south San Francisco Bay; they left when pollution finally destroyed the eel grass.

On the banks next to the road the wildflowers each spring compete with the birds for your attention—iris, checker bloom, chaparral pea, Indian paintbrush, California poppy, lupine. They bloom profusely among the herbs and grasses, inviting closer examination with a hand lens or at least a moment of distant admiration. On the road itself, you will probably see cottontail rabbits who have ventured out of the nearby coastal scrub for a look about and the promise of a meal. They will pause long enough to look at you before disappearing back into the bush. As you proceed along the road, grass gives way to brush—bush lupine, blackberry, coyote brush, bracken fern, thimbleberry, all typical species of the north coastal scrub.

You will shortly arrive at a large freshwater lagoon separated from the estero by a dirt weir or dike. Cattails and alders fringe the lagoon, along with blackberries, horsetails, lupine, and other plants, which together form a thicket between you and the water's edge. Coots and ruddy ducks

lurk about the cattails, but when they see you they will quickly swim toward the middle of the lagoon. The impossible chatter of the shortbilled marsh wren—a rapid buzz-whirr-whistle-chirp-cluck—provides the leitmotif for your visit, but the enthusiastic if sparsely gifted singer seldom shows himself from among the dense tule and rush.

Cross the dike to the narrow, but rapid outlet stream on the other side. Turn left along the stream, following a very narrow, overgrown path to a grassy bank, where you face this hike's moment of truth. In the late winter and early spring, when this hike is at its best, this creek is most likely to be difficult to cross, for then it is a rushing torrent that precludes any discrete wading. You must jump; and you must jump about ten feet in order to keep your feet dry. If you would rather not attempt the leap, you can walk back to the parking lot and from there explore the sand dunes of Limantour Spit and the birdlife of the lagoon, which provide ample compensation for not continuing this hike.

But if you decide to go on, take a long running jump and sail over the creek to the grassy bank beyond.

Follow the contour of the hills where they meet the salt flats, staying as high as the thick brush will allow. In the spring, you will see along this stretch the red and yellow flowers of the twinberry (*Lonicera involucrata*), a member of the honeysuckle family. At the first opportunity, when the bushes have sufficiently thinned out, head uphill, aiming for the highest point and avoiding thick brush. This stretch provides the greatest array and variety of wildflowers on the entire walk. As you wend your way through the sparse coyote brush, you walk through grasslands sown so thickly with buttercups and checker bloom that you scarcely know where to step for fear of reducing the display by even so much as a single bloom. Checker bloom (*Sidalcea malvaeflora*), the dusky rose flower that seems to be everywhere, is a member of the mallow family—of marshmallow fame. At first glance, you could mistake it for a godetia, or farewell-to-spring, but its five-petalled flower (the godetia has four) and its round serrated leaves soon identify it. A particularly striking wildflower along this stretch is the hairy star lily, or pussy ears (*Calochortus tolmiei*), a species of mariposa tulip. Its three pointed petals are held erect to form a bowl by three stiff sepals; a closer inspection shows that the purple petals are covered with white hairlike projections, giving the flower a shimmering effect. Few blossoms reward a close look with a hand lens like this one.

As you attain the crest of the broad rolling ridge, you will come to a grown-over ranch road. Do not follow it; continue straight ahead cross-country. Soon you will see a raw-looking road cut on the next ridge, some ways from you. Head for this until you can see the estuary below you, and a second lagoon, much like the one you encountered earlier, once again separated from the estuary by a dike. Head down and across the grassy hillside toward the lagoon. You will soon come to a steep-sided gulch, in which runs the outlet creek from the lagoon. Follow a faint path along the cliff's edge toward the water. Just before the lagoon, walk to the cliff's edge. You will see below you a board laid across the outlet creek. It is an easy scramble down the eroded slope to the crossing. On the other side, cross the dike and turn right on the old ranch road at the far end. It winds uphill, offering panoramic views of Limantour Estero, the ocean, Inverness Ridge far in the distance, and the large blue lagoon directly below you. Shortly this grassy track intersects another old road; turn right. It begins to drop toward the lagoon. You will see a single eucalyptus on your left, and beyond, a grove of about a dozen eucalyptuses near the lagoon. This grove, or the grassy slopes overlooking the water, offer a fine lunch spot, the best until you reach Muddy Hollow a couple of miles beyond.

Just before reaching the grove, look for an old, overgrown track heading uphill on your left. This is your route. (Do not take the road leading through the grove and down the draw toward the second lagoon in the distance, unless, of course, you merely want an interesting side trip.) The track uphill can be muddy going where it crosses a seep from a small pond just above the trail. Farther uphill, you will see a second small pond on your right. As you attain the crest of the ridge the track levels out, paralleling the lagoon for a bit before turning sharply left to meet a wide, gravel ranch road. Turn right.

Here on top of this ridge, your view is the entire compass: Inverness Ridge to the north and east, rolling hills to the north and west, due west the ocean and Point Reyes itself, to the south Limantour Estero and Drake's Bay. You feel expansive here, for you have room to expand; you could almost head off in any direction, just going with the contours of the land itself. But unless you are an experienced hiker and familiar with the area, resist the urge. The countryside, so deceptively congenial, can be tough going. Even if you do not get lost in the many similar hills and valleys, you will have a long overland bushwhack back to your car. Though the ranch road is by far the least attractive feature of the landscape, follow it up the ridge until it winds down in a valley to meet another dirt toad. Turn right on this road and walk downhill to where it crosses the creek that feeds into the large lagoon below. This creek supports a lush woodland dominated by old picturesque alders. A nearby grassy area is an inviting place to rest, and the trees themselves offer the first shade in some time, and the last until you get to Muddy Hollow.

The road crosses the stream on fill and heads uphill. On your right a grove of bishop pines grows on a knoll, the first pines you have encountered on this walk. From here on to Muddy Hollow you will see them scattered about the hills. Forming dense forests on the northern half of Inverness Ridge, the bishop pines seem to be creeping toward the ocean in many parts of the Point Reyes Peninsula. The ones along this trail look like the vanguard on this particular front. Related to the widely planted but, in nature, narrowly restricted Monterey pine, the bishop pine is found intermittently along the coast from Oregon to Baja California, often in extensive stands from San Francisco north.

Below the pines the trail runs beside a steep, eroded cut. Look closely and you will see many small holes in the sandstone. In the spring these provide nests for the rough-winged swallow, which swoops and chatters about the trail, often performing his aerial acrobatics just a few feet from your head. Other swallows found at Point Reyes include the barn swallow, violet-green swallow, cliff swallow, and purple martin. The rough-winged swallow is told by its brown back and white breast and belly.

Follow this road up over the ridge and down the other side. Do not take any of the side roads. You will see Muddy Hollow in the valley below. A dense stand of alders lines the creek, and a magnificent grove of cypress stands near the trail, just this side of the gate across the road. Walk around the gate to the Muddy Hollow parking lot and turn right on the trail signed to Limantour Estero. It is a mile and a half walk from here to your car through a dense woodland of alder and in open brush along the first lagoon you encountered on this walk. This whole stretch is alive with birds in the spring, especially during April and May, when visiting migrants drop into this lush valley before continuing their journey north. This is an especially fine place to look for warblers either in the spring or fall, including many rare eastern species that are seldom seen in other parts of the state. When you get to the dike, you will have come full circle, and your car is only five minutes down the road. On a busy Sunday the crowds of sunbathers walking up and back from the beach, laden with towels and radios and picnic baskets and sunburns, will provide a telling reminder of what you have missed by taking the Limantour Loop.

24. INVERNESS RIDGE

No less an authority than the former curator of botany at the California Academy of Science and author of *Marin Flora*, John Thomas Howell, has called the great Douglas fir forest of Inverness Ridge "the Black Forest . . . comparable in its development to the fir forests in Oregon and Washington." Though Douglas fir is common in the coastal woodlands of the Bay Area, it seldom forms pure stands like those of the Pacific Northwest. Usually it is only one of several species of forest trees, and it is often overshadowed, as in Muir Woods, by the statelier redwood. But on Inverness Ridge, the uplifted fault scarp that overlooks the Point Reyes National Seashore, Douglas fir is king, forming a dense forest adrape with moss and lichen and silent as an enchanted wood. The circular six-mile hike from Five Brooks Stables on old logging and ranching roads winds through one of the less-visited portions of this forest and culminates in the unusual Mud Lake, which has the appearance of a melted ooze of pistachio ice cream.

Except during the most inclement weather, this hike is good all year long. Even in summer, when fog invades the coast and hot weather the inland valleys, Inverness Ridge can provide an island of springtime weather. But the best times of year to take this walk are spring and fall. In May and June, wildflowers and fast-flowing streams make this a quiet paradise of iris, alum, sweet-scented bedstraw, and musky ceanothus—the treelike blue blossom, and other species that range from white to violet. For an autumn walk, choose late September or October, when the sky is intense blue and wisps of fog move only occasionally through the old man's beard that festoons the trees.

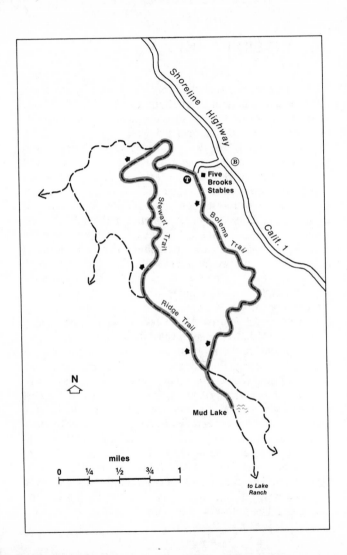

There are several good routes to Five Brooks Stables, depending on where you are coming from and how much time you have. All of them are beautiful, if somewhat slow country drives.

1. You can take the Mill Valley/Stinson Beach exit off Highway 101 just north of Sausalito and head west to Stinson Beach. Continue north on Highway 1 through Stinson Beach, past Bolinas Lagoon, and up the Olema Valley to Five Brooks Stables. On your left, a blue National Seashore sign, showing both horseman and hiker, marks the spot, which is five miles north of Bolinas Lagoon. This is the longest, if perhaps most picturesque route. Allow one and a half hours.

2. Turn off Highway 101 on Sir Francis Drake Boulevard. Head west through Kentfield, Ross, San Anselmo, and Fairfax, the last town of any size on this road. From Fairfax follow Sir Francis Drake for fifteen miles to Olema. Turn south on Highway 1. Five Brooks Stables is five miles south of Olema, on your right. Allow one hour.

3. Turn off Highway 101 on Lucas Valley Road, four miles north of San Rafael. Follow the signs to Nicasio and Point Reyes Station, which is nineteen miles from the freeway. From Point Reyes Station drive south on Highway 1 to Olema and Five Brooks Stables beyond. Allow one hour.

4. Take the Golden Gate Transit Authority bus 62 (Bolinas) from San Francisco and ask the driver to let you off at Five Brooks Stables. Catch the bus at the East Bay Terminal, at Fremont and Mission in San Francisco. For other city stops and for exact schedules, call 332-6600.

Even if the day starts gloriously warm, bring a sweater. Coastal fog, the sea breeze, and the deep shade of the forest can conspire to make it chilly in the Black Forest even on the sunniest days. A canteen of water is necessary any time of the year, for park officials advise against drinking from the streams. Bring a lunch unless you intend to travel light and eat later. Field guides to flowers and birds will prove useful.

Five Brooks Stables is a working farm that specializes in pasturing and renting horses. The only amenities for people consist of two Park Service latrines and a trail map with directions and mileage. You can use this to plan other hikes than the one described here. There is a medium-sized pond ringed with willows and equipped with two picnic tables near the trailhead. Though you will find better lunch spots farther on, the pond does give you a chance to see some mallards and coots close up. More interesting, perhaps, are the many species of wild birds that flit in and out of the willows and tall fennel.

Follow the *Bolema Trail* to your left (south). The park sign reads "Palomarin Trail" and has an arrow pointing left; this is the road to take. (The alternative says "Bear Valley" and points right.) Most of the trails in this southern portion of the seashore are old ranch and logging roads. There is a crying need to let these old tracks return to nature and replace them with more intimate and less intrusive footpaths. Yet for all that, the scenery at this end of the peninsula more than compensates the hiker for the unpleasing aspect of the trails.

As you pass wet marshy places, you can see where Five Brooks Stables got its name. Here you will find the slender red alder (*Alnus rubra*), which grows in dense thickets along the coast in moist bottomlands or along streamcourses. The slender gray-white trunks are reminiscent of birches, to which they are closely related. Their tiny cones hang down in groups of four and five. A pungent odor, which is too strong to enjoy, comes from the coast hedge nettle (*Stachys chamissonis*), which grows thickly at the base of the alders. This species of hedge nettle has fuzzy flowers of a dull lilac color. Unlike the true, or "stinging," nettle, the coastal hedge nettle has no stinging hairs. Two species of true nettle are also common in the area.

Hanging from the trees in great profusion is a vine that, in the fall, looks as if it is holding clusters of red caviar. This is the California honeysuckle (*Lonicera hispidula*), whose bitter scarlet berries brighten the woodland, more than making up for lacking the sweet perfume of its garden cousin. The wild honeysuckle grows rampantly on the trees of Point Reyes.

As you begin to climb the road, Douglas firs become more and more evident. The young trees are trimmed by browsing deer into odd topiary shapes, as if clipped by design for an ornamental garden. There is often a tall central stem surrounded by fluffed-out, bushy growth. The newest tips are trimmed off the side facing the road, perhaps because they are easier for the deer to reach. The dustier parts of the road show hoof prints all around these peculiarly shaped young trees.

When you come to the mature trees of the ridgetop forest, you will easily see how their size and weeping appearance could have suggested a hemlock to early botanists. Their botanical name, *Pseudotsuga menziesii*, reflects this early confusion and subsequent illumination: pseudotsuga means "false hemlock." Nor is this spendid tree really a fir. Its entire history is one of misnomers. The shapes of the mature Douglas firs on this ridge range from tall ship's-mast spires to grotesque specimens whose branches assume unusual forms. The lower branches tend to be bare of foliage, making this an open if completely shady forest. But when you stand on Inverness Ridge, you see how thick and luxurious the tree tops are as they tower overhead, with uppermost branches sweeping down, heavy with cones. In the nineteenth century both the redwoods and the Douglas firs of the Bay Area were heavily logged, including many of the Douglas firs of Inverness Ridge. But here many more survived, so that this forest, like the redwoods of Muir Woods, is a remnant that shows us what the woodlands around the bay must have once been like. Occasionally, on one of the rutted side roads on Inverness Ridge, you will see stumps black with age and overgrown with huckleberries or poison oak; but logging is nowhere evident, and the general effect is not one of rawness, but rather of an open park, where the trees that were spared reach great heights.

The dead Douglas firs that remain standing in the forest provide havens for woodpeckers and other hole-nesting birds. Woodpeckers have also riddled the live trees with tiny holes in their incessant search for insects and grubs. You are likely to see only two woodpeckers in this forest—the downy and hairy—but a third, the fabulous pileated woodpecker, a crow-sized bird with a prominent scarlet crest, has been sighted here from time to time. Tree swallows also nest in these woods, as well as that larger swallow, the purple martin, which is rather uncommon in the Bay Area. In the spring watch for black-headed grosbeaks warbling from the treetops. The most common bird of the forest is probably the Stellar's jay, the large crested bird with feathers of true Prussian blue. Other year-round residents include the brown creeper, an odd little bird that

winds endless spirals up the tree trunks in search of insects, and the red-breasted nuthatch, whose high, hornlike call is a constant sound in the forest. Other common birds to look for are the ever-present chestnut-sided chickadee, the ruby- and golden-crowned kinglets, and the giant black raven. Overhead, look for hawks, turkey vultures, and white-throated swifts, one of the fastest birds in the world.

About the time you think you should be reaching the top of Inverness Ridge, 1,300 feet, you still have a way to go. A small sign directs you to ignore the trail straight ahead, which is marked by a sawed log, and continue up the curving, wider road to the top. From time to time you can see the farms of the Olema Valley below you. The hills on the eastern side are gentle and accented by darker patches of woodland in the canyons.

As you move closer to the ridge top you may see wisps of fog and smell the ocean to the west. Along the road are the dark scat of raccoons and foxes, both of which are common in this forest. The sides of the banks of the trail are tunneled with the holes of pocket gophers. Everywhere you can see the tracks and traces of animals, but only the birds show themselves.

At the top you come to a crossing of several trails. On a hot day, this is a good place to stop and rest your back against a tree trunk and look up into the mighty Douglas firs. A map and sign at the junction indicate that you may continue straight ahead to join the *Coast Trail* at Lake Ranch or turn left and head for the *Palomarin Trailhead* (4.7 miles) via the *Ridge Trail*, which is a good walk if you have arranged for transportation at that end (see Section 25). If you turn right, you can walk to Glen Camp (4.2 miles), where overnight camping is available by reservation only, and eventually swing back to the Bear Valley Trailhead (4.6 miles beyond Glen Camp.) Again, this is useful only if you have arranged a car shuttle.

But if your car is back at Five Brooks Stables and you do not wish to retrace your steps, turn right on the Ridge Trail and walk about three-quarters of a mile to pick up the *Stewart Trail* back down to the ranch. This makes about six and a half miles in all, with the last part of the walk downhill. But before heading back, follow the trail leading straight ahead at the junction for a quarter mile to Mud Lake, about as unlikely a place as you can expect to find at Point Reyes.

On the short walk down to the lake the Douglas firs seem even larger and more impressive, perhaps because they are on the moister seaward side of Inverness Ridge. An immense floor of ferns slopes up on your left, and on your right, California laurels—completely covered with a green moss that hangs about an inch from every branch—rise from an understory of huckleberry.

Sometimes an almost phosphorescent alga covers the surface of Mud Lake. The center of the pond is filled with tall rushes; its shore is ringed with sedges as well. During the spring birds are plentiful, but in the fall the silence of the scene is broken only by the croaking frogs. As you walk around the lake, they will leap into the water, but you may see only the splash. Look for animal tracks in the mud. This place would be a prime hunting spot for raccoons and a watering hole for deer.

Back at the junction, turn left on the Ridge Trail. Shortly you will come to a meadow, which in the spring is filled with poppy, lupine, and checker bloom. Covering perhaps ten acres, the meadow is a perfect resting and picnic spot.

During the fall it is brown and dormant, waiting for the first winter rains to start the cycle of green again.

After about a mile of rather open country, you leave the gravelly road for a foot trail that takes off to the right. It is not marked by a sign, but so many feet have followed this path that you will find it with no difficulty. It is always a relief to have your feet touch the soft duff of a forest trail after walking on a hard road. The scene becomes more initmate as the track narrows to a thin thread winding through the woods. Cut off your mind from the outside world and let your senses absorb the stillness and fragrance of the forest. The smell of the laurels is especially strong and as two streams flow together the fallen leaves of buckeye and a big-leaf maple make a golden carpet. Much too quickly, this little forest bypass ends at which you follow downhill to your right.

Along the streams and wet places on this walk to Lake and back you may notice elk clover (*Aralia californica*), which grows thickly and rapidly, reaching so from seed in a mere ten months, only thereafter. In the summer the plant is topped globes of flowers, which enliven the stream October is its most striking season. The replaced by a striking plum-purple berry. aralia in many places are the red and which also sport bright berries.

You will arrive back at Five Brooks or four hours after beginning this walk many trails at Point Reyes, but now it so easily as on this walk through Douglas firs grow in such spl silhouetted against the blue sky

25. THE LAKE RANCH

The Lake Ranch is named for five freshwater lakes that occupy depressions behind the rubble of ancient landslides. It is quite unlike any other part of Point Reyes National Seashore, but its peculiar charm does not lie merely in the lakes themselves, but in the picturesque juxtaposition of ridge and valley, forest and grasslands, intimate ponds and the vast sea. Despite the ranch road, which is your trail on most of this hike, and the old ranch buildings, the place seems frozen in time, as if in coming here you had traveled into the past. On a foggy day, when mists embrace the black forest of Inverness Ridge and turn the sea cold gray, the landscape looks like something from a fairy tale. When the sun shines, the country is decked with jewels, shimmering waters and the emerald or gold of the hills.

From the *Palomarin Trailhead* at the southern end of the Point Reyes National Seashore it is a two-mile walk to the Lake Ranch and another two miles to Double Point. By arranging a car shuttle you can walk all the way to the *Bear Valley Trailhead*. This strenuous twelve-mile walk can be made in a day by experienced hikers, but most people will prefer to take two days, spending one night at Glen Camp. Advance reservations are required for overnight camping. Another shuttle can be arranged between the Palomarin Trailhead and Five Brooks Stables. At Lake Ranch, the *Lake Ranch Trail* forks to the right, climbing up the ridge to Mud Lake (see Section 24) and from there down to Five Brooks Stables. The total distance is just over seven miles.

From San Francisco, drive north on U.S. 101 to the Mill Valley/Stinson Beach exit (Highway 1). Drive west for one-half mile to an intersection with a traffic light, where

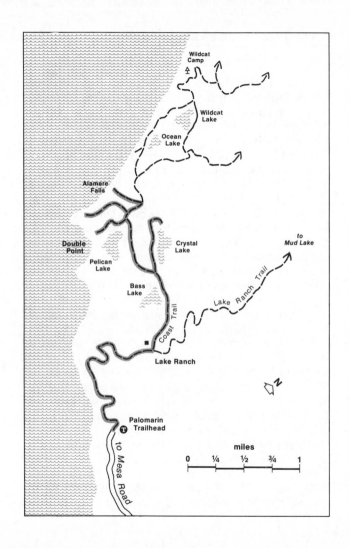

Wildcat
Camp

Wildcat
Lake

Ocean
Lake

*to
Mud Lake*

Alamere
Falls

Double
Point

Crystal
Lake

Pelican
Lake

Lake Ranch Trail

Bass
Lake

Coast Trail

Lake Ranch

N

Palomarin
Trailhead

to Mesa Road

miles

0   ¼   ½   ¾   1

you turn left. Drive about three miles to the Panoramic Highway junction. Keep left, following the sign directing you to Stinson Beach. Continue past the town of Stinson Beach for five miles, where, at the head of Bolinas Lagoon, you turn left on the Olema-Bolinas Road. Just before reaching the town of Bolinas, turn right on Mesa Road. Follow Mesa Road out into open country. It passes an old ranch in a protected gully before coming to the radio towers on the cliffs overlooking the ocean. Here the road gets rougher as you enter Point Reyes National Seashore. Follow the road past the Point Reyes Bird Observatory on your left to a large parking lot and the Palomarin Trailhead. A sign at the trailhead gives mileages to various points.

Although you will find lots of fresh water along the trail, none of it is potable, so take your own. You will also want to take advantage of the several outstanding places to eat lunch along this walk, so pack something special and try to choose between the forest-rimmed waters of beautiful Bass Lake and the sunny grasslands of Double Point, to name only two possibilities. Much of the year this coast is either foggy, windy, or both; the exceptions are few. Dress warmly for this hike. You can always shed some of your clothes later if you happen to hit a hot day. Either hiking boots or good walking shoes are satisfactory for this trail.

The best times for this walk are either spring or fall. The weather is best in September and October, and the wildflowers are best in March and April. Summer days are frequently overcast, and winter days are blustery and cold. But if you dress appropriately and know what to expect, this walk can be superb in any season. It has its fine points even in a December drizzle. If possible, take the hike on a weekday, when the sense of solitude is overwhelming. You can always find your own lonely spot, even on Sundays.

The trail begins under an old grove of eucalyptus in a field full of thistles and coyote bush. If you are a birdwatcher, you may get no farther than a few feet before taking your first pause. Lesser and American goldfinches, house and purple finches, scrub jays, Bewick's wrens, wrentits, Allen's and Anna's hummingbirds, red-winged blackbirds, white-crowned and song sparrows, and various other birds can be expected in this area.

The trail descends into a shallow gully and up the other side to the flat mesa. At first you walk through an open grassy area, but this soon gives way to coastal scrub as the terrain becomes steeper on the right side of the road. This scrub is like a miniature forest, with shrubs in place of trees and an understory of annual and perennial herbs. Among the more common shrubs are coyote bush, California sagebrush, bush monkeyflower, California honeysuckle, coffeeberry, and poison oak. In all, some two dozen species of shrubs grow in the coastal scrub of Marin County. This trail is a good place to become familiar with most of them.

The first part of the trail sticks closely to the edge of the cliff. In places you can peer directly over to the water below. There is little or no beach between Double Point and Bolinas Point to the south, so along this stretch the waves break directly at the base of the cliffs. The odd-looking brown blobs in the water just offshore are the floating bladders of kelp. At first you may think these bobbing brown algae are a raft of sea birds, but a quick look through the binoculars will show otherwise. But you may see real sea birds floating among the seaweed, including surf scoters, white-winged scoters, western grebes, and gulls. Occasionally you may be treated to the exceedingly strange sight of a great blue heron standing on one of the floating masses of kelp. Gulls love to ride the rising currents of air that form when a strong offshore breeze bounces upward off the vertical cliffs. Depending on the season, you may see western gulls, herring gulls, California gulls, Heerman's gulls, and Bonaparte's gulls. Identifying gulls is an arcane skill that even many avid birdwatchers have not mastered, so don't feel bad if you cannot tell many of them apart.

Not far from the trailhead, the trail turns away from the cliff's edge to drop to a small creek in a deep ravine. As you move inland into the moister, more protected habitat, you will notice that the vegetation changes. Willows form thickets along the stream. Look for yellow monkeyflowers by the small pond near where the trail turns back up the other side of the ravine toward the coast. Wilson's warblers and orange-crowned warblers are common among the willows in the spring. The latter's song is a repetitive, undistinguished trill from the undergrowth.

The road continues along the cliffs for a short way before turning inland a second time. This ravine is much wider and deeper than the first, and you can see the road as it winds for about a mile up the opposite slope to a small notch several hundred feet above and about a mile away. This notch is the narrow gateway to the Lake Ranch, which lies just a short way beyond in a picturesque basin between the wooded Inverness Ridge and the grass- and shrub-covered hills along the coast. From the coast, you head inland, dropping to a small creek flowing down the ravine. Again, willows grow thickly along the watercourse. The road crosses the stream and heads toward the coast for a short distance before turning back and starting its long, winding course to the notch above. The walk up is steep, but not too steep, and there are several places to stop and rest. In March, Douglas iris are plentiful, coming in several shades of blue and purple. Morning glory trails in rank profusion over the shrubbery, and bright paintbrush, yellow, red, and orange, grow along the roadside with California poppy and lupine. There are several grassy spots on the way up where you can sprawl out and take in the vista. This deep, wide ravine, with its almost constant updrafts, is a good place to watch for hawks.

From the notch, where steep cliffs rise on either side of the road, you can see for the first time on this walk the majestic Inverness Ridge, with its dark mantle of forest extending down moist canyons toward the sea. On the more exposed slopes, the forest gives way to grasslands and scrub. On your left as you descend the isolated little ''valley'' opens out. Soon you can see a couple of small ponds, which host a few wild ducks in the winter. Finally, the old white ranch house comes into view, along with a couple of dilapidated outbuildings. At the bottom of the grade you will come to a fork in the trail and a sign pointing left to Coast Camp, 18.5 miles. The right fork is the Lake Ranch Trail to Mud Lake and the Ridge Trail. Take this fork if you are hiking to Five Brooks Stables. If you are hiking to Coast Camp or the Bear Valley Trailhead, or if you plan to continue to Double Point, turn left at this junction, passing a small pond and a tall hedge in front of the old house. Shortly beyond, you will come to an open gate across the road. Begin climbing a gradual grade, at the summit of which the most beautiful of the five lakes, Bass Lake, comes into view. On a sunny day its shimmering blue waters surrounded by Douglas fir will make you think you are somewhere in the mountains rather than a mere half mile from the sea. There is a picnic table at the lake, and unless there are people everywhere, this is the best spot to eat lunch. The southeast shore of the lake is thick with alders, and here and there it is fringed with cattails. Some people carry in small rubber rafts for paddling about the lake.

If Bass Lake is too crowded for your taste, continue uphill on the road. Before long, notice a faint trail leading to a low notch in the wooded ridge on your right. This trail leads to Crystal Lake, a hidden gem where you can find a measure of solitude even on crowded days. Since it is nowhere visible from the main trail, few people visit this open, marshy lake. There are excellent grassy spots around the lake for spreading out your lunch.

Continuing on the main trail, you soon come to Pelican Lake, made famous by Philip Hyde's photograph in the Sierra Club book, *An Island in Time*. With little effort you can discover pretty .much where the photographer stood. Across the lake is the narrow V-notch in the ridge, where the lake's only outlet stream drops to the sea. On a bright afternoon, when the sun is out over the ocean, you might even be able to see the same spangles on the water. Pelican Lake has no pelicans—at least not anymore—but it is a sure-fire hangout for gulls. They fly in from the ocean through the notch and settle down in noisy crowds on the calm protected waters of the lake. Here they seem to spend much of their time splashing about, with wings aflap and bodies thrashing in the afternoon bath. They are seldom still; some are leaving as others arrive. Some circle overhead, squawking and generally carrying on in their familiar rowdy fashion. Yet for all that, they are exquisitely beautiful and wild, the purest white on the brightest blue at one of the most enchanting spots in the Bay Area.

The road stays high above the lake (there are a couple of trails down to the shore), crossing over a saddle on the low ridge between Pelican Lake and Alamere Creek. From here you can look up the narrow canyon down which the creek flows from Inverness Ridge. It is an enchanting chasm, steep-walled and heavily wooded with Douglas fir. No trail leads up this canyon, and perhaps that, more than anything else, makes it especially alluring. It looks deliciously wild, as if it might hide secret places of exquisite beauty that few Sunday hikers have beheld. A short side trip to the mouth of the canyon can be made by following a rough trail of sorts that branches off to the right after you have descended from the saddle to the moist flat below. You can cross the creek on a narrow log and walk along the base of the distant ridge back to the Coast Trail.

Continuing along the main trail, you descend easily to the junction with the trail that leads out to Double Point. If you have the time, it is worth the walk. Except on very windy days, the north point is a fine place to sit. You have glorious views of the ocean and the coast, from south of San Francisco to Point Reyes, across the water to the northeast. Double Point really is two distinct headlands. They are separated by a small sandy cove much favored as a resting place by Stellar's sea lions. You can see why. Surrounded by steep cliffs, they offer these animals a perfect retreat from any real or imagined enemies, including man himself.

Back on the Coast Trail, continue on to Alamere Creek and follow it down to the cliff's edge to see the falls. In winter or spring, when there is a lot of water in the stream, the falls are an impressive sight as the stream plunges straight down in a fifty-foot free-fall to the sand. The most impressive waterfall at Point Reyes, the Alamere falls is visible on a clear day from Point Reyes and the headlands of Drake's Bay across the water. There is no easy access to the beach from here, and the cliffs are dangerously unstable, so heroic attempts to descend to the sand could be unfortunate. It is far better to content yourself with sitting at this overlook, enjoying the sound and fury of the stream and the sense of being in the middle of nowhere.

You have now hiked about four miles, so this is a good place to turn around and head back to the car. But if you have the time and the stamina, you can continue on the Coast Trail for another half mile or so to see the last two lakes of the Lake Ranch. These are Ocean and Wildcat lakes, just beyond which is Wildcat Camp, the overnight camp at the seashore especially reserved for organized groups.

Having hiked into the Lake Ranch and Double Point, it is sure to become a place you will return to again and again, if only to savor in each season and in all weather its enchanting blend of water and woodland, its glorious vistas, and its aura of mystery and time out of mind.

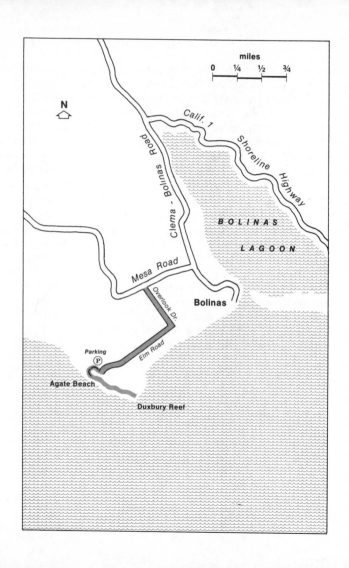

26. DUXBURY REEF

Duxbury Reef, a marine terrace composed of shale, chert, and sandstone, is located just off Duxbury Point at the extreme southwest corner of the Point Reyes Peninsula. It lies outside the Point Reyes National Seashore and is administered by the California Department of Fish and Game. If you are fascinated by tidepool life, you should by all means visit the reef, but *do not disturb the tidepools or collect any specimens*. So many collectors have already raided the reef that it has lost much of its former richness. Even so, it is still an outstanding place to observe the myriad forms of life that inhabit the intertidal zone. Local residents in nearby Bolinas have confessed to regularly taking down signs leading to the reef in order to protect it from further depredations. But there is no reason you should not enjoy the reef so long as you are willing to obey the sign you see as you approach the reef. It says: *"Tidepool life is fragile, take nothing but pictures."*

From San Francisco, drive north on U.S. 101 to the Mill Valley/Stinson Beach exit (Highway 1). Drive west for one-half mile to an intersection with a traffic light, where you turn left. Drive about three miles to the Panoramic Highway junction. Keep left, following the sign directing you to Stinson Beach. Continue past the town of Stinson Beach for five miles, where, at the head of Bolinas Lagoon, you turn left on the Olema-Bolinas Road. Just before reaching the town of Bolinas, turn right on Mesa Road. At Overlook Drive, turn left; then turn right on Elm Road, which leads to the parking lot above Duxbury Point and Agate Beach. To your right is a short dirt trail leading down to this enormous shale reef. Remember two things for your visit: (1) find out when the tide is especially low so that you can walk almost a mile out to sea on the slippery rocks; and (2) wear hip boots, or old tennis shoes that you can throw away, since the salt water will pretty much rot them. Also, prepare to dress warmly because you are out on a point of land that catches every sea breeze on this routinely windy coast.

This walk below the high-tide line should be a leisurely one, for there is no better way to see the odd, colorful world of the tidepool than by just squatting down and patiently watching. These are miniature worlds, where small details tell important stories, where shy creatures scurry into dark holes at your approach. Crabs, of course, are the most mobile of the tidepool creatures, at times frustrating even the most patient observers. Often lurking in cracks in the rocks or half buried in sand, crabs wait for the tide to wash in bits of dinner. If you are lucky they may eventually emerge long enough for you to identify them—if you bring along a good field guide to seashore life. At Duxbury Reef you may spot several species of crab, including the purple shore crab (*Hemigraspus nudus*) and the larger common rock crab (*Cancer antennarius*), an orange-brown relative of the deep-water commercial crab.

As you walk over the reef you may notice the curious red algae called "sea nipples" or "dead men's fingers" (*Halosaccion glandiforme*), which grow in small groups and look like deformed rubber gloves. You may also find a few purple sea urchins, those lovely pincushions of the tidepool whose beauty persists after death in the form of their exquisite empty cases. Far out on the reef, near the brown sea palms, you will find some of the oldest forms of life, the chitons. Seemingly immobile creatures, they have nevertheless been known to return to their territories if moved a reasonable distance away. Although there are many species of chitons native to this coast, you are most likely to see the black chiton (*Katherina tunicata*), *Nuttallina californica*, and *Mopalia muscosa*. But be forewarned: these mollusks are difficult for the amateur to identify.

As you explore the reef, don't let your fascination with the tidepools blind you to the magnificence of sea and sky and cliffs. To the north rises the heavily forested Inverness Ridge, and west of that, across Drake's Bay, the granite prominence of Point Reyes stands boldly in the sea. Due east, the western slope of the Tamalpais highlands rises steeply above Stinson Beach, the ridges falling off sharply to the south before gathering once more to form the steep-faced Marin Headlands. Beyond lies San Francisco, the northern tip of the long peninsula whose rugged western coast you can see far to the south on a clear day. On the clearest days, you can even see the Farallone Islands interrupting the southwest horizon.

As long as you are momentarily distracted from the living drama of the tidepools, take the opportunity to examine your fellow travelers on the reef—not the people, but the birds. Four unusual members of the sandpiper family (*Scolopacidae*) make it their business to poke about reefs and rocky coasts for food, and during the spring or fall migrations you might easily find all four attending your walk. The most common—indeed it can be seen in this area the year round, though only very rarely in summer—is a small black and white bird that you will probably first notice only as an unexpected movement on the reef, as though a piece of rock had suddenly detached itself and scampered a few feet. This is the black turnstone, a squat, short-legged bird about the size of a robin. Usually your second glimpse will reveal not merely one bird, but several, for these turnstones commonly congregate in small busy flocks that seem to leave no crack unprobed as they scurry about the reef looking for dinner. When they fly they cease suddenly to blend with their surroundings, presenting to the viewer the dramatic black-and-white motley of their wings and tails.

Closely associated with the black turnstone, indeed often feeding with it, is the surfbird, which looks remarkably like the turnstone except for its yellow legs and lighter bill. In flight, it lacks the striking wing pattern. The surfbird nests in the vicinity of Mount McKinley during the summer, but for the rest of the year spends virtually all of its time probing the rocks and reefs along the Pacific Coast from southeast Alaska to South America. Similarly, the black turnstone nests in the arctic tundra even though it is almost never found inland during the rest of the year.

The third sandpiper you may see on the reef is the wandering tattler, which is uncommon even during migrations. But if you are lucky enough to spot one, you will recognize it by its bright yellow legs and comic habit of bobbing as it walks, as if the rhythm of life was a rumba beat. Although it eschews the company of other tattlers, preferring to dance alone, it is occasionally seen in the company of surfbirds and turnstones. Like these two, it nests in the far north.

The fourth sandpiper is the rarest of the reef birds in this area. Though a few are seen each year in the Bay Area, the rock sandpiper seldom strays south of the Oregon coast during its winter retreat from central Alaska. It closely resembles both the surfbird and the turnstone, and to be certain of identifying this rare visitor you will need the services of a good field guide. (If you ever spot a rock sandpiper, the local Audubon societies would appreciate hearing about it.) All four of these species share in common dark brown or gray backs, which, of course, provide perfect camouflage for their rocky habitat, but make distinguishing them difficult except for the practiced birdwatcher.

Overhead, you can pick out a number of different species of gulls, depending on the time of year. A particularly striking sight during the spring is to see a large flock of Bonaparte's gulls on their way north to the breeding grounds. A small gull that hovers and dives like a tern, Bonaparte's gull is the only common species on the California coast that sports a solid black hood during the spring and summer. In the winter they are common throughout the Bay Area, but retain only a small black spot behind the eye as a reminder of their summer splendor. Other gulls to look for include the western gull, ring-billed gull, Heerman's gull (dark gray with a bright red bill), herring gull, California gull, and glaucous-winged gull. People who lump all these and other species of gulls under the partly inaccurate term "seagulls" usually are surprised to discover that there are, in fact, so many different kinds. The Bay Area, for example, hosts some ten species during various times of the year.

When the ocean begins to lap at your feet, it is time to turn around and head back toward the shore. But if you can, search the eel grass for nudibranchs, the brightly colored sea slugs that move with such grace that you may never tire of watching them. It is thought that the bright colors of the nudibranchs function as protective coloration of an odd sort, in that would-be predators may thereby be frightened off. If you ever see one of these fringed jewels, you are not likely to forget it.

As you approach the shore, examine the tidepools once again just in case you missed something on your way out. If you see the black and silver turbans of the tegula snail moving about with unaccustomed speed, you can be fairly sure that a hermit crab (*Pagurus hemphilli*) has taken over the empty shell as a temporary home. Most of the body of the hermit crab is inside the shell; only the front claws and eye-stalks are visible. As the crab grows, it must find a larger shelter for itself, and sometimes there is a good deal of squabbling among hermit crabs for housing rights. If you lift one from the water, it will retreat as far back as possible, and when you replace it in the tidepool, it will frequently lie still for a minute or two before scuttling off.

The tidepools of Duxbury Reef are rich vessels of life that deserve our care as well as our attention. They provide instruction as well as delight and satisfy that urge in all of us to uncover the unexpected and marvel at the bizarre. To stop and admire and then to leave undisturbed, to enjoy without possessing—these are unaccustomed responses for too many people. But they must become fixed habits for all of us if the glorious tidepools of the California coast are to retain their richness for even another generation.

27. BARNABE PEAK

Samuel P. Taylor State Park is not part of the Point Reyes National Seashore. It is included in this section of the book because of its proximity to Point Reyes. It offers the only overnight campsites in the area accessible by car. This makes it a popular stopover for people visiting the national seashore. But it should also be savored for its own special attractions, and these are best experienced by walking, whether it be the short loop to Stairstep Falls (see a park map) or the seven-mile loop to Barnabe Peak described below. Samuel P. Taylor State Park is a jewel for the hiker because its trails are less traveled than those of other parks in Marin County. Just why this should be is puzzling since it is a well-known picnic and camping spot.

The hike to the top of Barnabe Peak is one of the finest anywhere in the Bay Area. During the spring wildflowers bloom profusely along the trail; the woods, grassland, and coastal scrub support a large variety of birds; and the views of west Marin are unsurpassed even from the top of Mount Tamalpais, which is much higher but several miles to the southeast. Although the entire loop is seven miles long, it is not a difficult hike so long as you follow the route described below. From the wooded canyon of Paper Mill Creek, you climb several hundred feet to the top of Barnabe Peak, but the grade is steep only for a short way. Most of the hike is done on a delightful, narrow path that makes a long, gradual traverse of the southwest ridge leading up to the summit. It is appropriately named the *Ridge Trail*.

Plan on taking most of the day for this hike. Samuel P. Taylor State Park is about an hour's drive from San Francisco, and the loop trip to Barnabe Peak will take you

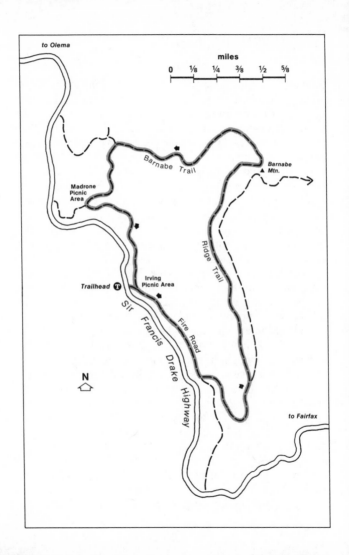

to Olema

miles

0   1/8   1/4   3/8   1/2   5/8

Barnabe Trail

Barnabe Mtn.

Madrone Picnic Area

Ridge Trail

Irving Picnic Area

Trailhead T

Sir Francis Drake Highway

Fire Road

N

to Fairfax

about four to six hours, depending on how long you take to rest, study the birds and flowers, and eat lunch. You should definitely carry some food and water on this walk; much of the trail is uphill in the sun, and you will want refreshment at some point along the way. For the same reason, you should avoid this trail on the hottest days. Pick a sunny day when a breeze is blowing in off the Pacific. Fortunately, such days are common throughout the year in the Bay Area. Unlike the great majority of walks in this book, this one is well away from the influence of the ocean, which means that it is a good choice when other areas are fogged in. By the same token, if it is warm right on the coast, it is likely to be downright hot at Samuel P. Taylor State Park. Despite the length of this hike and the fair amount of climbing involved, you do not need heavy-soled boots; good, comfortable walking shoes of any sort will do quite well.

From San Francisco, drive north on U.S. 101 to the Sir Francis Drake Boulevard exit. Turn off the freeway and follow the signs to San Anselmo. After passing through the towns of Kentfield and Ross, you will come to a rather complicated intersection in the town of San Anselmo known as "the Hub." Here, Sir Francis Drake Boulevard goes straight ahead, making a left turn after the stoplight. Follow it through the town of Fairfax, shortly after which the road begins to climb over a low but steep-sided ridge. From here the road drops into the San Geronimo Valley. Passing the golf course in the middle of the valley, continue through the villages of Forest Knolls and Lagunitas, right after which you enter a canyon densely forested with redwoods. You will pass a number of private cottages tucked in the woods along the creek. After you cross a bridge, you enter Samuel P. Taylor State Park. After crossing a second bridge, look for a dirt road immediately on your right. Turn in and park where you can. The trail begins to the left of the dirt road near a sign that reads: "No Parking, Fire Lane." Another sign identifies the broad dirt track as the Ridge Trail. You are at the Irving Picnic Area; your route follows the road leading off to the right from the signs at the trailhead.

Although most of this walk is through the bright, open grasslands and scrub that sweep down from Barnabe Peak, this first stretch runs through the lush mixed woodland of Lagunitas—or Paper Mill—Creek. Groves of fine redwoods are interspersed with stands of laurel, tanoak, madrone, and California buckeye (*Aesculus californica*). Related to the horse chestnut of the east, this beautiful tree is common in the inland portions of the California Coast Ranges, where it thrives on arid slopes, amidst the scrubby blue oak-digger pine woodlands. In Marin County it tends to prefer the more arid hills and valleys away from the coast, though it is not averse, as here, to a well-watered canyon. The buckeye is the first deciduous tree native to California to lose its leaves—usually by late August—and the first to get them back—no later than February. It is a beautiful tree in any season, but especially in late spring and early summer, when it sports huge spikes of creamy white flowers. You can recognize it at other times—except in fall and early winter—by its lovely compound palmate leaves.

As you walk along the fire lane you can see the stream below you to the right. Although Lagunitas Creek has water in it all year round, it is notably sluggish during the summer months. In the winter, however, it can be a raging torrent. Big-leaf maples and alders prefer such moist streamside habitats as this. When you climb away from the creek, you will leave these two beautiful trees behind. The alder, a

steep-sided, grassy peak to the north along the ridge. The west slope of Barnabe Peak drops abruptly down to the canyon below. Your route will traverse this slope (you might even be able to make out the faint horizontal trace that marks the trail) and wind around the west side of the peak to a fire lookout on the peak just behind it.

Continue up the ridge through the coastal scrub. If you make this walk in the spring, you will notice that the California poppies seem to be larger and more abundant than they were below. Some specimens measure three to four inches across. Surely this poppy must set some sort of standard for the color orange—it seems the very paradigm of orange. The blossom is saturated with the color, and next to it all other native flowers pale. Others are as beautiful, perhaps, but none is brighter. Because of its beauty and because it is common throughout most of the state, it is fittingly designated as the state flower of California. In the early days, before grazing had drastically altered most of the state's native grasslands, the California poppy was even more abundant than it is today, turning whole fields orange each spring. There are still a few places where you can see it in its former glory, but they are rare. Even so, it remains one of our most common native flowers, adorning not only our grasslands, but decorating such man-made wastelands as old road banks and vacant lots. It has the particularly charming habit of often teaming up with lupines; their combined blue and gold make one of the most striking bouquets provided by nature.

A new wildflower makes its appearance along this stretch of the trail. This is the curious fiddleneck (*Amsinckia* spp.), a coarse, weedy member of the borage family (which includes the Pacific houndstongue) that is common both inland and along the coast. It takes its name from the way in which its flower spike unrolls from the bottom up, giving it a coiled appearance similar to that of the neck of a violin. The common shrub along the trail is coyote bush. You will also see some coast sagebrush. Old man root sprawls along the trail and through the shrubs.

Stay on the road until you see a sign on the left that says "Ridge Trail." Here your route leaves the road, which continues up the crest, to follow a narrow path that traverses the west side of the ridge. Although you can get to the top of Barnabe Peak by continuing up the road, it is an inferior route to the trail. The road is less well graded, being an alternation of steep ups and downs, with a few fairly level stretches tossed in; it lacks the breathtaking views you get from the trail; and it is less intimate, less wild in its mood, than the narrow path. It is also hotter because the broad, flat-packed dirt reflects more heat than do plants. So by all means choose the trail, but before leaving the road, climb up the bank on the right side for a splendid view of Lagunitas, the San Geronimo Valley, and the ridges of eastern Marin County.

For all its virtues, the trail presents two minor hazards to be aware of and avoid: poison oak and ticks. Poison oak is related to the poison ivy and poison sumac of the East, and shares with them the annoying property of causing most people to break out in red, itching blisters. The best way of recognizing it is by its leaves, which are similar to those of some species of oak in having several rounded lobes, and which usually, though not invariably, grow in sets of three. They are green, tinged with red, in the spring, green in the summer, and crimson in the fall. In the winter poison aok loses its leaves, but even the stems and branches can produce a reaction. Since the overwhelming majority of shrubs to be found in this area retain their leaves all year, a good rule of thumb in the winter is to avoid any bare-stemmed bush or vine. Poison oak intrudes onto the trail at several points; you can avoid it by being watchful. If you are among the unfortunates who break out in blisters merely by being too close to the plant, by all means forego the pleasures of this trail and take the road. Should you accidentally come into contact with the plant, wash with soap and water at your earliest opportunity.

Ticks are a little harder to avoid. These tiny parasites look like little crabs, having the same sort of flattened body and straddle-legged stance. They inhabit the shrubbery, dropping onto their victim—a deer, a man, a dog—when he passes by. They sense their target by its body heat. Once on the skin, they burrow their minute heads into you and proceed to feast on your blood. You can't simply pull them out because as often as not the head will stay behind in the skin, making for a nasty infection. If this happens, see a doctor, who will be able to remove the rest of the beast. There are various theories about how to remove ticks—sticking a hot match to their rear ends, screwing them out with tweezers, and others—but one of the best, though not foolproof, methods is to apply petroleum jelly to the tick. If you're lucky, he will surface for air and you will be able to pluck him off. It is not a bad idea to carry a little petroleum jelly and some tweezers in your daypack if you plan to do much hiking through tick country. As you walk along this trail, periodically check yourself and your companion(s); once you leave the scrub for the open grasslands of the upper slopes of Barnabe Peak, you can relax.

The Ridge Trail climbs gradually to the summit, rounding the west face of Barnabe Peak and heading toward the second peak and the fire lookout. Below you on the left, you can see a fire road winding through the grassy hills: this will be your route back. You meet the fire road at the saddle between the twin summits of Barnabe Peak. At the junction there is a sign that merely says "trail." Turn right on the road and in a few yards, just before you reach the fence, turn left on a trace heading off through the grass. This leads up to a hiker's stile in the fence. You come out at the lookout.

On the right side of the building there is a flat spot to sit and eat lunch. From here, the view is panoramic. Straight across from you is the Bolinas Ridge stretching south to the Tamalpais highlands. The highest ridge to the west is Inverness Ridge, the backbone of the Point Reyes Peninsula. It is easily recognized by its thick forest cover. The highest peak you can see on the ridge is Mount Wittenberg. The peninsula stretches off to the north toward Tomales Point, and just this side of the ridge lies the long finger of the sea known as Tomales Bay. The hills on this side of the bay are predominantly covered with grass. The prominent ridge thrusting up all by itself to the northwest is Black Mountain, which, being almost entirely given over to grasslands, is either green or gold, depending on the season. Before leaving the summit, walk to the opposite side for a fine view of the San Geronimo Valley. Far to the southeast you can see the summit of Mount Tamalpais and the radar domes on the ridge leading up to the peak. The body of water nestled in the wooded canyon below and to the south is Kent Lake.

From the summit, retrace your steps back to the fire road and follow it to the west. It drops very steeply, and you will quickly understand why you do not want to take this road up to Barnabe Peak. In about one and one-fourth miles, you will come to a second road leading off sharply to the left. It is marked by another brown post with a yellow tip; again there is no sign. Directly below you are the highway and park maintenance buildings. Turn left at this junction, and when you come to another post, stay left again. The trail to the right leads down to the parking lot at the Madrone Picnic Area. After walking through open grasslands, you will pass a water tank on your left just before entering the woods, where the trail drops steeply downhill toward the highway. When you come to another post, just before you reach the highway, turn left and cross the creek. Shortly the trail will veer to the left to cross Barnabe Creek. Notice the abundant maidenhair ferns that grace the bank on your left after crossing the creek.

From here, the trail runs level through the woods, paralleling the highway below. Just before reaching the Irving Picnic Area, the trail drops down closer to the road. Keep left and in a few yards you will come out at the parking lot where you began.

Bibliography

RECOMMENDED FIELD GUIDES

Braun, Ernest and Vinson Brown. *Exploring Pacific Coast Tide Pools*. Naturegraph Publishers. Healdsburg, California. 1966.

Brown, Vinson *et. al. Handbook of California Birds* (Enlarged Second Revised Edition). Naturegraph Publishers. Healdsburg, California. 1973.

Dawson, E. Yale. *Seashore Plants of Northern California*. University of California Press. Berkeley, California. 1966.

Ferris, Roxana S. *Flowers of Point Reyes National Seashore*. University of California Press. Berkeley, California. 1970.

_____ *Native Shrubs of the San Francisco Bay Region*. University of California Press. Berkeley, California. 1971.

Geary, Ida and Al Philpott. *The Leaf Book*. The Tamal Land Press. Fairfax, California. 1972.

Grillos, Steve J. *Ferns and Fern Allies of California*. University of California Press. Berkeley, California. 1966.

Metcalf, Woodbridge. *Native Trees of the San Francisco Bay Region*. University of California Press. Berkeley, California. 1970.

Munz, Philip. *Shore Wildflowers of California, Oregon and Washington*. University of California Press. Berkeley, California. 1964.

_____ *Spring Wildflowers of California*. University of California Press. Berkeley, California. 1964.

Orr, Robert T. and Dorothy B. *Mushrooms and Other Common Fungi of the San Francisco Bay Region*. University of California Press. Berkeley, California. 1971.

Peterson, Roger Tory. *A Field Guide to Western Birds*. Houghton Mifflin Co. Boston. 1961; paper edition, 1972.

Robbins, Chandler *et. al. Birds of North America: a Guide to Field Identification*. Western Publishing Company. New York, 1966.

Sharsmith, Helen. *Spring Wildflowers of the San Francisco Bay Region*. University of California Press. Berkeley, California. 1965.

Watts, Tom. *Pacific Coast Tree Finder*. Nature Study Guild. Berkeley, California. 1973

FOR FURTHER INFORMATION

Bakker, Elna: *An Island Called California*. University of California Press. Berkeley, California. 1972.

Gilliam, Harold and Philip Hyde. *Island in Time*. Sierra Club. San San Francisco. 1962; revised edition, 1974.

Howell, John Thomas. *Marin Flora*. University of California Press. Berkeley, California. 1970.

Mason, Jack (with Helen Van Cleave Park). *Early Marin*. House of Printing. Petaluma, California. 1971.

_____ (with Thomas J. Barfield). *Last Stage for Bolinas*. North Shore Books. Inverness, California. 1973.

_____ *Point Reyes, the Solemn Land*. North Shore Books. Inverness, California. 1970.

McMinn, Howard E. and Evelyn Maino. *Pacific Coast Trees*. University of California Press. Berkeley, California. 1967.

Murie, Olaus. *A Field Guide to Animal Tracks*. Houghton Mifflin Company. Boston. 1954.

Ricketts, Edward F. and Jack Calvin (3rd edition revised by Joel Hedgpeth). *Between Pacific Tides*. Stanford University Press. Stanford, California. 1939; 3rd edition, 1960.

Smith, Alexander H. *A Field Guide to Western Mushrooms*. University of Michigan Press. Ann Arbor, Michigan. 1975.

SIERRA CLUB TOTEBOOKS®

The Best About Backpacking, edited by Denise Van Lear

Fieldbook of Nature Photography, edited by Patricia Maye

Huts and Hikes in the Dolomites: A Guide to the Trails and Huts of the Italian Alps, by Ruth Rudner

Reading the Rocks: A Layman's Guide to the Geologic Secrets of Canyons, Mesas and Buttes of the American Southwest, by David A. Rahm

Foot-Loose in the Swiss Alsp: A Hiker's Guide to the Mountain Inns and Trails of Switzerland, by William E. Reifsnyder

Starr's Guide to the John Muir Trail and High Sierra Region, by Walter A. Starr, Jr.

Wilderness Skiing, by Lito Tejada-Flores and Allen Steck

Hiking the Yellowstone Backcountry, by Orville Bach

Hiking the Teton Backcountry, by Paul Lawrence

Climber's Guide to Yosemite Valley, by Steve Roper

Cooking for Camp and Trail, by Hasse Bunnelle with Shirley Sarvis

Food for Knapsackers, by Hasse Bunnelle

Hiker's Guide to the Smokies, by Dick Murlless and Constance Stallings

Hut Hopping in the Austrian Alps, by William E. Reifsnyder

Hiking the Bigfoot Country, by John Hart

To Walk with a Quiet Mind, by Nancy Olmsted

The Climber's Guide to the High Sierra, by Steve Roper